SMALL BUT MIGHTY

Abby,
   Thank you so much
for your support & feedback.
Your comments put the whole
work in a new direction that
increased its saliency. I hope
I reflected your vision well.
                    Amy

SMALL BUT MIGHTY

Changing the World Through Consulting

Gary Romano

ISBN-13: 9780692762479
ISBN-10: 0692762477
Library of Congress Control Number: 2016912582
Civitas Strategies, Lynnfield, MASSACHUSETTS

Contents

Acknowledgments

The roots of this work span my entire career. I've been influenced by many thinkers, but those with the greatest impact have been a set of clients, colleagues, and, in many cases, I am proud to say, friends who have taught me immeasurably about the craft and business of nonprofit consulting, specifically Lindsey Allard Agnamba, Tony Berkley, Toni Dunbar, Jillian Hasner, Judy Jablon, Khaatim Sheerer El, Gabrielle Miller, and Don Pemberton.

I've been on a mission since September 2015 to publish this book, and I owe a debt of gratitude to the Civitas Strategies team. Alison LaRocca served as an intellectual foil and partner from initial concept to writing, pushing back on my ideas to make them stronger, helping me to continuously clarify concepts to be accessible to all readers, and encouraging me to complete the book. Lindsey Kotowicz repeatedly refocused me on the needs of my core audience and message, while Stacia Silvia masterfully edited the manuscript from my garbled dictation.

Fran Simon, the founder of Early Childhood Investigations Webinars (www.early-childhoodwebinars.com), graciously agreed to a four-part webinar series on the book. She not only helped in getting the concepts presented out to consultants early, but she also provided a critique that was valuable in the final iteration.

Last, but certainly not least, I want to acknowledge the influence of my family and thank them for their support. My boys, Ben and Finn, have taught me about what life's priorities are—in terms of not only work/life integration but why I want to wake up every day and contribute to the greater good for the sake of everyone's children. My wife, Karen, continues to be my primary partner in my personal life but also in my professional one. She was a crucial influence not only in the creation of this work but in every consulting gig and business decision I've made. I wouldn't be the father, husband, or consultant I am without her.

As you read this book, what is valuable should be attributed to those mentioned here, and any flaws are entirely mine.

Introduction

This book is not for everyone.

This book is for aspiring or established consultants focused on helping the nonprofit and government organizations that are trying to improve our world.

Chances are you have expertise in some form of social impact, such as education, human services, or policy advocacy. What you don't have is experience in starting and building a business.

You're not alone. Every month I'm contacted by leaders who want to make the jump into consulting and learn how to start their firm as well as by existing consultants who want to grow their organizations.

If you are one of these people, this book is for you—I am glad you are here. The nonprofit world is using consultants more than ever, and recently established technologies help you share your talents and, in turn, have social impact to an extent that has never been seen before. The same market demand and technology also creates the possibility of stronger lifestyle integration, and consulting can be a prime vehicle for realizing these benefits.

But you are also moving in a market that is very different from that faced by most consultancies. Resources are tight, and your customers' values are fundamentally different from those in for-profit markets. Accordingly, launching and building a consultancy serving nonprofits can be a difficult endeavor.

Further, most consultants fall into one or more of four archetypes, each of which increases the likelihood of a failed business: Hesitater, Top Heavy, Temp, and Hamster.

The Hesitater is the person who considers making the leap to consulting but never actually does it. Hesitators have skills that other organizations could benefit from, but they aren't sure how to start their businesses—not just creating the corporation itself but pricing services, getting clients, and sustaining their enterprise. Since they don't know where to start, they continue to churn, failing to ever actually start their businesses and complete the leap into consulting.

The Top Heavy is on the other end of the spectrum, finding two or three other senior-level peers to partner with in their consultancy. The rationale is usually that having only (or almost exclusively) senior staff will draw clients in since they will only deal with the principals. The Top Heavy also tends to take on all the trappings of a traditional consultancy—finding an office and bringing on an administrative assistant. The result is a consultancy that looks a lot like a big organization right from the start. However, Top Heavys' lack of attention to developing a sustainable business model means that in the near or long term, their bloated organizations implode under the weight of overhead.

The Temp is half in and half out of consulting. One of the first things I recommend to any mid- or senior-level nonprofit professional who has been laid off or left a job without another in hand is to become a consultant. It gives you something to add to your résumé and generates income while you search for another job. Unfortunately, Temps tend to react quickly and jump into consulting without thinking about how they will do it or for how long. They typically get work but usually undersell themselves and take on projects that are too short (ending before they find more work) or too long (they have to leave for a full-time job before their client commitment is completed) and for too low a fee (since they aren't thinking about a long-term business, just immediate cash flow). The result is usually frustration for themselves and their clients as they work hard on projects while job searching, doing neither particularly well.

The Hamster is by far the most common archetype. The Hamster is the quintessential solo practitioner—doing it all, from managing the phones to watching the books to serving every client to writing every document. Usually Hamsters fall into consulting because of an outside trigger. Often they were laid off and wanted something to do while looking for work or didn't like where they were working and wanted to make a rapid move into something different. The origin isn't the problem; their challenge is that they never stopped to think about what their business would require. They usually dive into the first contract and do it all themselves. They add another project or two and soon find themselves doing everything to keep up with the work.

They are unable to stop and figure out how to get the help that could make their lives easier. Hamsters typically survive year after year, but like a hamster on a wheel, they are constantly overworked and exhausted from having to do everything, and they never quite make enough money or have the time to engage support.

You can try to avoid being these archetypes by systematically building a business. There are a lot of great general small-business books, organizations out there to help you start up a business, and even a small number of books specifically for the consultant. But what isn't out there is a guide for aspiring or current consultants working with nonprofits who want to wed their consulting work with child-and-family or community, state, or national impact and are facing tight budgets and profit margins not seen in typical consulting.

ENTER CIVITAS STRATEGIES, LLC

I am often approached by nonprofit leaders wanting to start their own consultancy because, over the past twelve years, I have moved through the very obstacle course that they now face: first working at a small consultancy and then starting and building my own.

I started my firm, Civitas Strategies, in 2010. The organization's mission is to help public-service organizations, for-profit and nonprofit, increase their social impact through highly effective strategy advisement, coaching, and evaluation. Our clients include a number of the "usual suspects" of the nonprofit world—foundations, nonprofits, and community-based organizations. But from our first year, we have received referrals for clients we never anticipated—other consultants. These referrals have continued to come in month after month and year after year. They all come for the same reason—though there are a number of consultants they can turn to for business advice, they need not only the business acumen but also someone who understands the challenges and opportunities of the nonprofit world (i.e., navigating a market with tight margins and a commitment to social impact).

Originally, my advice to these clients was ad hoc, but it eventually grew into one of Civitas Strategies's formally provided services. I drew on more than twenty-two years of consulting experience with nonprofit and government agencies, communications and project-management skills developed over six years in the for-profit science and engineering field, and success in launching four start-ups (two nonprofits and two for-profits) to help my clients navigate the challenging world of launching and sustaining nonprofit consultancies.

What started as a few clients quickly grew to include not only paid projects but also monthly referrals for no-cost support to help experts launch their first nonprofit consultancies. In the feedback I received, I realized that I had inadvertently created, tested, and refined a simple process that consistently helped aspiring and current consultants rapidly clarify their vision of service and craft a sustainable business model to realize it.

SMALL BUT MIGHTY

Once I developed this process for nonprofit consultants, my challenge was sharing it. As a small consultancy ourselves, our reach is limited by design—I have limits on the number of clients I'm able to serve each year. I wrestled with how I could reach more of the people who were seeking our advice. That led to this book, *Small But Mighty*, and the associated website (smallbutmightybook.com), which will allow you to start and build your own social-impact consultancy. I have organized the steps needed to start your consultancy into four sections: "Get Started," "Get Customers," "Get Help," and "Get Growing."

In "Get Started," I will help you clarify your mission, uncover your value (what customers will get from working with you), and discover your unfair advantage (what gives you an edge over competitors). In short, I will establish the foundation on which you will build your consultancy. I will then take you step by step through creating your minimum viable company (MVC). The MVC comes out of the lean-thinking movement, which was first captured in Eric Ries's book, *The Lean Startup*. Lean thinking is not about doing things on the cheap but rather moving as quickly as possible to deliver your product and service. Included in this is the idea of the minimum viable product, where instead of building a full product from bumper to bumper, you build just enough to start talking to customers about it or making sales and then flesh it out over time. I've adapted this idea to creating your company and providing a path to establishing the minimum legal structures and infrastructure you need to start consulting and bringing in revenue. The MVC is also expandable, so as you grow over time, so can your company.

Now that you are up and running, you need to "Get Customers." This section will take you from the first customer in the door to creating and maintaining a pipeline of customers who will sustain your consultancy over time. At the heart of the approach is the Bull's-eye, a simple way to drive your sales and marketing activities by the probability of and time to sale. (Note that I put "sales" first. You'll learn more about that in this section too.) The basic premise is one that is tried and true in sales—your current and former customers are your best prospects for continued engagement. That being the case, I will still talk about how to efficiently expand your customer base to new people. I will also introduce the Pemberton Method of tracking your prospective clients to help you know if you are chasing too few or too many potential projects. You will also learn how and when to add new products and services. Finally, I will talk about how you continue to build value and relationships with your customers by regularly listening to their feedback and needs.

There is a difficult balance between not taking on outside support, be it contractors or employees, and taking it on too quickly. In "Get Help," I will review how you should assess your needs for outside help so that you can add it in ways that will leverage your time and keep your organization profitable. In discussing outside help, I will talk not only about more junior people and consultants but also about when to bring more senior people or full partners into your consultancy. You will also learn about how to develop a talent pipeline—to find the best people to work with you without having to invest a huge amount of time and effort. Once you have talent, there is the question of how you develop it. I'll present an observational method of training that enables you to not only develop skills in supporting staff but also ensure they understand the culture of the organization.

No matter how much planning you do, nothing actually happens until you execute. "Get Growing" will help you set goals and objectives and incorporate them into a simple "control panel" format that will guide your efforts year-round. I will also talk about how difficult it is to find mentors (though they are very valuable) and how to instead create a community of peers to help you keep on track and address the many challenges that come up in running a business. This section will also provide other supports you can access to help you develop yourself and your organization over time.

Ultimately, this book is only valuable if it moves you from plan to action—this is not a theoretical endeavor. As you go through each section and each chapter, I have included exercises so that you can immediately apply the information to building your consultancy. I strongly encourage you to complete each exercise and also to treat this book as a workbook—making notes throughout that will help you move as quickly as possible from your ideas to a viable consultancy.

Section I: Get Started

In this section, we are going to go from your idea about what your consultancy can do to having a clear mission to drive your organization and generate substantial value for clients.

I want to start off with a concept that should travel with you through this book and the development and growth of your consultancy—lifestyle design. The term "lifestyle design" was coined by Tim Ferriss in his book, *The 4-Hour Work Week*, and is an evolution of life/work balance, pushing you to actually design your business model to also fit your personal needs, rather than fitting a personal life around work requirements. The ability to engage in lifestyle design can be one of the greatest personal benefits of consulting.

I'm not only a believer in lifestyle design but also a practitioner. The year I founded Civitas Strategies also marked the year our first child was born. When my wife went back to work after maternity leave, I began to have a day a week at home with our son (which continued with our second son). At first it was very hard for me to say no to my clients and tell them I wasn't available on Mondays—I had always prided myself on being the person they could rely on to get things done no matter what. But I soon realized this was a core feature of how I wanted to shape my business model. Have I lost some work? Yes. But far less than I feared, and it doesn't come close to the joy of the time I've had with my boys.

To be clear, lifestyle design is not about balancing life and work but rather about life/work integration, building the structures you need to be satisfied with both and conveys how they interplay with each other rather than trying to segregate them.

As you build your business model and your minimum viable company, I want you to keep all three of these concepts in mind. Think about how you will generate the greatest value and do it in a way that will provide a profit to sustain your business while designing it to meet the needs of your whole life, not just your work life.

STARTING WITH THE END IN MIND: MUST-HAVES/MUST HAVE NOTS

I am a true believer in Stephen Covey's maxim, "Start with the end in mind," and I consider the "end in mind" to include what you want out of your venture, both personally and professionally. Throughout this book, I'm going to repeatedly mention the opportunity you have for lifestyle integration—to shape your business model so that it meshes with your professional and personal goals. Like any element of your business model, this execution may not be flawless. At times you'll have compromises on one side or another, but without lifestyle design you are almost assured conflict within your life and competing priorities.

EXERCISE ONE: MUST-HAVES/MUST HAVE NOTS

Set aside about forty-five to sixty minutes, alone or with your significant other (since his or her lifestyle is affected by yours), and articulate what your business must accommodate—for both your professional and personal life.

- **Step One: List Your Must-Haves**—What are the five or fewer things that you definitely want to include in the design of your organization? These can be personal, such as having the afternoons as open as possible to spend time with your child, or professional, such as working exclusively in vulnerable communities or within a specific sector.
- **Step Two: List Your Must Have Nots**—What are the five or fewer things that you consider outside the limits of your firm and work? For me this was significant travel (I limit myself to no more than fifteen days a year), yet I continue to work in geographies across the United States. This could also be professional—for example, I know one consultant who didn't take on particular types of early-learning projects because she didn't think they were effective and didn't want to devote her time and effort to them.
- **Step Three: Know What You Are Willing to Put at Risk**—The reality is, no matter how confident you are and no matter how many customers are lined up waiting for your firm open, small businesses are risky. I give aspiring consultants the same advice I used to give casino visitors when I was living in Las Vegas: only put at risk what you're absolutely willing to lose. However, to be clear, you need to be specific about this up front. In the case of money, you want a budget. Similarly, with time, you want to give yourself permission to spend the amount of days and hours a week that you're willing to invest to create your organization.

When I created Civitas Strategies, I found myself with a varied list of must-haves and must have nots, including having a day a week with my son, working with vulnerable families and children, having a desire to include pricing that could accommodate all types of organizations in the mix (from large foundations to community-based nonprofits), and planning to work at home (not because of convenience but because of wanting to keep costs as low as possible).

I was willing to put at risk four hours a week and live solely on my wife's salary for six. By the time I opened my doors, it was evident my risk was already mitigated, but it was important for me to know what I was willing to sacrifice up front.

Keep your list handy throughout the time you're reading this book. If you're reading this in electronic form, use the note function of your reader so you can refer back to it when you want to. If you have a hard copy, write it in the back of the book. As we go through subsequent exercises and think about your business, you'll want to take this out as a clear reminder of how you may want to integrate your life.

Finding Value and Mission

To craft your mission, you must first understand your value. From the moment clients first decide to pay you for a project, every client decision is driven by the value you produce. This is particularly true when you're serving nonprofit organizations, because typically they believe they're making a decision between funding a consultant and funding a family or child. The value you produce has to outweigh the impact of using these resources to directly fulfill their mission.

Since your value generation is so crucial to the success of your consultancy, I'm going to spend a lot of time focusing on it. I'll start by sharing a simple way to find your value and then hone in on the most crucial elements and the niche you should serve. I will also discuss how to incorporate into your value the differences in your work versus competitors. Then, I will talk about how to take all the data on value and craft a mission that's inspiring not only to you but also to potential clients.

WHAT IS VALUE GENERATION?
To understand the idea of value generation, I first need to talk about the "six-letter word" of the nonprofit consulting world—profit. I hope I didn't make you uncomfortable using such vulgarity, but if you're going to have a viable consultancy, you're going to have to get used to the word. In fact, this is one of the most important concepts you will read about in this book and something you should be constantly thinking about in every decision you make. I've found that, particularly in the public consulting world, profit tends to be an uncomfortable subject—not only for clients but also for consultants who are cognizant of their clients' particularly tight funding and resources.

Let's be clear—profit is not evil; it is an important part of your business model. Profit is just the difference between what clients are paying you and what it costs you to serve them. For example, if a client pays you $10,000 and it costs you $8,000 to do the project, your profit is $2,000. But this isn't necessarily what you pocket. Your profit is needed to pay for sales and marketing, development of your capacity (e.g., that training you want to attend), unforeseen events, or capital investments (like a new laptop to replace your clunker). In short, without profit, your organization can atrophy and implode.

Your profit is also critical insurance against the lean times. The reality of consulting is that no matter how good a job you do, there will be slow times. Maybe a few projects all end at once, or some clients run into delays in having the funding needed to engage you. I'll talk about cash flow later in section three, but know that your clients' payments may not line up with your expenses (a nice way of saying the cash may not hit your account as fast as you need to write checks). Accordingly, I cannot recommend strongly enough that you keep some of your profits in reserve for the lean times. Surprisingly, most consultants withdraw all their profits as fast as possible, causing headaches later on.

Profit is also part of your compensation—and there is nothing wrong with that. Remember, you are taking a risk by being a business owner. There's no guarantee that the clients will keep coming in. And if your business fails, there's not a severance package to tide you over or insurance to compensate your loss. What you have put into your business can be lost. Therefore, profit is also part of your compensation for putting your money and reputation at risk.

Last, and certainly not least, your profit isn't always going to be positive, and this should be a great concern to you. A negative profit margin means you're actually losing money on your products or services, which can be the fastest way to having to close your doors. I've found that rarely do nonprofit consultants run a consistent negative profit margin. Instead, more commonly, there is one large project that gets underestimated and overworked to a point where it pulls down your overall profitability. The result is that the one project can start to suck resources from other projects, leading to underservice of your other customers and serious, if not irreparable, damage to your consultancy.

Value generation needs to be at the heart of your business. Put simply, this is what you are creating for your clients—how you're solving problems and helping them realize opportunities. I've found that consulting is often held in just slightly higher esteem than lawyers in our society. The problem is not the industry per se, but rather that people invest a fair amount of their resources when they engage a consultant and often do not get lasting value out of that experience. This is a particular problem when you're working with nonprofit organizations, since they have few resources that are not already going to the families and children who need their help. As a result, nonprofit organizations are hesitant to engage consultants; they are fearful that they won't get any value out of the investment.

Accordingly, you need to be driven to understand how you are going to provide value, large or small, for your client. To see your value, you need to focus on the outcome or result, not the service. Following are some examples of a service and the value it produces.

Service	Value
Advocacy	Favorable policy change
Coaching	Stronger, more confident leadership
Data Analysis	The ability to make decisions based on data and not guesses
Evaluation	An understanding of what is working, what isn't, and how to be more effective
Fundraising Counsel	Increased revenue
Strategic Planning	A clear pathway to the future

Here's a more extended example. Our first service at Civitas Strategies, and a continued core offering, is strategic and growth planning. Strategic planning can be a tough market. When I talk about client disappointment in consultants, everyone has a strategic-planning story involving wasted time and money. You know the one I mean—where everyone got very excited during the planning process, but when it was done, they had a beautiful plan that they never used again. Once in a while, they would look at the plan sitting up on the bookshelf and lament about what a waste of time and money it was.

I wanted our clients to have a different experience from the get-go. I talked to a number of nonprofit and government leaders and also drew on my own experience in the field. And I realized one of the differences between plans that sat and those that moved was a clear transition from planning to execution. In reaction, I insisted that every strategic and growth plan Civitas Strategies creates include a clear pathway to execution in the first six months that details, for each strategy, what needs to happen, who needs to do it, and in what time frame. This seemingly minor innovation unlocked huge value for clients—they now could actually move from creating a plan to realizing it.

On the other end of the spectrum, consider the many small things you can do to generate value for your clients. In my organization, we are constantly looking for ways to connect people within our network. We are very careful about these connections, thinking ahead of time about the value for both parties. But the simple networking can help our clients identify dependable vendors, potential funders, and others who will help them realize their goals. Our clients continually appreciate these connections. Though they are small, they do provide significant value by advancing their mission.

UNCOVERING YOUR VALUE

Over the years I found that, particularly in the nonprofit sector, professionals tend to be modest about what they do and the value they generate for others. That often means this first step—finding your value—can be a particularly difficult one. Even without modesty it's a difficult task, since people rarely say "here's how you provide value," and, at times, the value you think you are producing may not be the same as what your clients see.

I found the most direct way of learning about your value is by talking to current and former clients. Most clients will not have consciously thought about your value until prompted. But it's worth the prompt—at least it will reassure you about what you believe your value is, and more than likely it will result in a few surprises or a different way of looking at the value you generate.

I'm using a very broad definition of "client" here—many of you have not been in consulting or had any sort of market transaction for your services. Instead, your clients may be organizational or system leaders, your own executive director or leadership, external partners, and others. That is, people who have used the product or service you want to bring to your consultancy.

EXERCISE TWO: COLLECTING DATA ON YOUR VALUE

1. Start the process of finding your value by making a list of five to fifteen clients (current or former) that you believe have found value from your work. Again, these could be colleagues, bosses, or even subordinates. If you are already a consultant, include lapsed clients on the list—this is a great way of reengaging them, and their insights can be invaluable.

    If possible, include a broad array of clients so you have multiple perspectives. Ask yourself the following questions to ensure you have the mainstays as well as the outliers:

    -   Do you have clients for your bread-and-butter work? (If you are an existing consultant, this is the way you make most of your revenue. If you are just starting, these are clients who you believe your consultancy will rest on.)
    -   Do they cover representatives of both large and small projects?
    -   Do you hit the major and minor topic areas you serve?
    -   Does the list include different types of organizations (that can be based on their size, complexity, or other characteristics that are relevant in your work)?

2. Next, come up with your questions. You'll want to keep the conversations to less than an hour (ideally thirty to forty-five minutes), so try to keep it to three or four questions. Most basically, you want to ask how you produce value. But it is also important to learn where you could have generated more value and how you compare to other options (i.e., your competition).

    Here are some sample questions.

Aspiring Consultants

-   When I have worked with you, what have you found to be my greatest strength or contribution?
-   What do I do that is at the top of the field or that you don't see from my peers?
-   What have been my greatest achievements?
-   If I started a firm and only offered three services or products, what should they be?

- Which firms and consultants do you use now? Why do you work with them?
- What keeps you up at night? What are your driving concerns?

Established Consultants

- Why did you select me to work with you initially? If they have renewed— Why did you choose to use us again?
- How have I most benefited your organization?
- Who are my competitors? Who is being engaged to do the same or similar work? What are the criteria leaders are using to make those choices?
- What can you get from me that you don't get from other consultants?
- What could I do better?
- What service or product do you wish I offered?
- What keeps you up at night? What are your driving concerns?

I have two thoughts on the questions. First, there are not many of them— that's because of the time constraint (limiting the conversation to thirty to forty-five minutes).

Second, if you can, use an intermediary—someone who is not you, since this may open up the opportunity for clients to be more honest about where you haven't been as successful. Intermediaries can also provide great perspective on clients' answers, since they are somewhat removed from the equation.

3. Send out an e-mail to each interviewee and book the interview. The e-mail can be short, but you do want to be up front with them. Start with why you are doing this (either to find your value as you start your organization or, if you are already a consultant, to find how you can generate greater value). If you are using intermediaries, introduce who they are and that they will be conducting the interviews. Then describe the time commitment (thirty to forty-five minutes), and close with reminding them how valuable you know their time is.

4. After you complete each interview, send a thank-you note—even if by e-mail only. Yes, this is obvious, but it is important enough to add. The interviewees are giving you crucial data that will build your business; the least they deserve is your written gratitude.

There are some exercises you may want to skip, but my strongest recommendation is to do these interviews. They are absolutely crucial. Some of you are going to be afraid of how clients would react to your request for the conversation. I can tell you from experience that they will be receptive. Over the years, my firm has performed thousands of interviews like this on behalf of our clients, and I can only think of three instances where I was denied. In those cases, there had been a severe issue between the interviewee and our client, which I knew ahead of time and was aware that securing the conversation would be a long shot. Much more typically, your clients will feel flattered that you want to include them in the development of your enterprise or increasing your level of impact.

It is crucial to do these interviews not only at the start of your enterprise but also on a regular basis. I check in with clients and former clients at least every six months and probe for value—they're not long conversations, but I always learn something really important.

I have two additional thoughts on the interviews. First, whenever possible, have the conversations in person or using videoconferencing (like Zoom, which is free or inexpensive, depending on your needs). A significant part of human communication is nonverbal, so you can learn a lot by watching how your interviewees act and react. Second, remember that this is ultimately a listening exercise. You need to focus on what they are saying, not what you want them to say or your reaction to it. Sometimes negative feedback can make you defensive. Here, you need to exhibit extreme composure.

The following is part of a conversation on value I had recently with a former client. I have removed identifying and privileged information.

Me: I really enjoyed the work we did last year with your strategic plan—I felt like you got a lot out of it and you were really positive at the end of the project. I'm thinking right now about how I can improve our effectiveness at Civitas Strategies and provide greater value for clients. What did you find was of greatest value for you and your organization at the end of the project?

Former client: That we use it! Seriously, we do a lot of these plans every year for different programs, and this is one of the few that we've actually kept using. It's great that we can keep coming back to it.

Me: I'm curious, why did you hire us? You have a lot of different choices.

Former client: It was because of Barbara. (Who is Barbara? Is she a former executive director? Does it matter?) She spoke so highly of you, and we really love the work that she's done as a partner. Knowing that you could get the job done was a big deal for us.

As you can see in the short vignette, I like to get right to the crux of the conversation. I also garnered other information, such as why they chose us over other options. And I found out I have another champion for my work! After the call, I made sure to thank Barbara; I continue to keep in touch with her regularly in case she can refer me to others.

HONING IN ON YOUR VALUE

Now you need to distill your value. Start by going through your notes of each conversation and writing the key ideas that were presented. Write each point of value down. There will be a lot at first, but don't be overwhelmed. We'll be cutting them down.

For the analysis, go to a place where you can focus. Turn off the phone and your e-mail—I know being disconnected can be unnerving, but this is a crucial, fundamental part of creating your consultancy and one that necessitates focus. Divide your list by value generated directly (such as helping a client solve the problem or meeting a critical need) and value that differentiated you from the competition (such as your pricing or similar previous projects you've worked on).

Next, take your points and consolidate them by combining multiple points of value that really are expressing a larger idea. For example, one fund-raising consultant I know was told that she always knows what to say to a foundation funder to secure a grant, and another client told her that she has an uncanny ability to know which funders are the best choices. Those could be two separate ideas, or you could say that she deeply understands how foundation staff are motivated and make their decisions.

Once you have your points whittled them down, begin to prioritize them based on your sense of how much the client's benefit was derived from each. This will be a difficult task, since this is more about your gut impression than a hard-and-fast rule. I've found that sometimes a top point of value is the most popular one (i.e., the one most frequently mentioned); other times it can be something mentioned only once, but it would be highly valued by other potential clients.

Also, look for surprise value. I've found in our work that about 80–85 percent of what you hear is what you expect to hear (value you thought you were generating but is now confirmed). But there is typically a hidden 15–20 percent that will be unexpected, and often this surprise value will have outsized impact on how you see yourself and your work. This is what you aren't articulating to prospective customers but should be.

Keep working on your list until it is down to five to seven points. This number is roughly the number of items you can keep in ready memory—and your value will come up again and again as you talk to clients or prospective clients. You want them to be ideas you can easily keep top of mind. Once you have your five-to-seven points of value, share them with a small number (two to five) of *critical friends*—people you trust and who will be honest with you. These could be social friends, coworkers, your employees, or even a long-time client. Ask them what they think—if this list is reflective of their experiences with you. This will refine your five points further—maybe adding one or eliminating another or just changing their wording. This is a critical final step that is worth taking before you move forward and build your business around these values.

Here's an example of the original feedback received on a project (adjusted to protect confidentiality) and how it was distilled down in two rounds.

Interview Feedback	Distillation 1	Distillation 2
• "They help us see the forest for the trees." • "When the initial report came back to us, we realized we had seen the landscape all wrong and now we understood what was really happening." • "They saw things in the data that we didn't even realized were there- the result was a whole new perspective on our environment."	• Seeing forest for the trees • Unique perspective on and insights about the environment	Provide our clients the ability to see what everyone else is missing.
• "When an unforeseen event happened, they were able to roll with the punches without missing a beat." • "We didn't realize until later that we were a moving target- we kept changing what we wanted but they kept up with us." • "There was a point where they were very honest about the project being off-track and how we needed to make adjustments to have the results we wanted."	• Rolled with the Punches • Saw when a pivot was needed in a project	Adeptly adjust to changing circumstances to ensure your needs are met

DEFINING YOUR NICHE

Now that you have recorded your value, we will focus on finding your niche—the specific space you want to work in. This may not be your only niche, but it is important to have specificity in where you start to work. Especially since, if you are starting out, you have no sales and marketing staff beyond you. You will be living by your wits, so it is crucial to focus the time you have hunting for work.

Most consultants in start-ups don't think about this. Instead they think broadly, asking themselves, "Who is everyone in the universe who may buy what I am selling?" This can be a very exciting question to pose.

A few years ago, one of my clients posed this question at a group planning session. Four of us were together, with me in the facilitator role. The goal was to identify how they could grow a service for schools that showed great promise in improving academic outcomes. The question garnered a lot of excitement, and the answer took on a life of its own. Before we knew it, we were talking not only about schools but about districts, state government, and even the federal government through a large-scale public-policy play.

I was finally able to rein in the group. They had provided excellent arguments as to why all these potential customers would be interested in their service. However, they didn't have unlimited resources or even a large sales staff (they actually had no sales staff at all—the CEO led the organization and also conducted all sales activities). Further, they lacked relationships with the people who would be crucial to making these sales; even if they did pursue the strategies, it would be a long-term play.

As the group realized how difficult it was going to be, they became deflated and overwhelmed. I was able to pivot them to focus on what they could pursue with their current resources and connections. There still was an exciting market opportunity, and it was one that could not only build near-term growth but also move them in the direction of some of these larger strategies for the long term.

It may feel good to know that there are a lot of possible clients out there, but in practice I've found it leads to inaction. With so many possibilities, the novice consultant chases them all and moves few to sale. With specificity about your potential market, you gain clarity about where to put your sales and marketing time. It doesn't preclude you from taking on a client in another niche, but it does mean being proactive in a limited space first.

When I talk to clients about defining their niche market, I challenge them to use the "room constraint." That is, to define a niche where everyone could be in one room—be it a living room or a concert hall. The key is being able to say that they all fit in that space.

I came on the idea years ago when I was working on a project for a large foundation, helping them to design a national math and science initiative. In talking with one expert, I asked why his organization was focused on improving the skills of principals instead of teachers. His answer was that the team working on the initiative realized that all the principals in the United States could fit into a football stadium, but all the teachers could not. In other words, they could reach the principals since it was a number they could get their arms around. In contrast, the number of teachers was overwhelming, and it appeared that reaching all of them would be impossible. Similarly, I challenge you to do the same.

Here are some examples of actual niches we have heard in our work:

- We help leaders of small- to midsized foundations identify ways to improve education systems.
- Our firm focuses on advising administrators in small charter-school networks throughout New England.
- I advise large foundations that want to improve child-welfare systems on the most significant policy and advocacy plays they can make.

Before we dive deeper into filling your room, let's talk about who you may want in the room—your potential customers. Your customers must have the three Rs: reason, responsibility, and resources. They need a reason to hire you—they have a pressing need that you can fill or a problem you can solve. This may seem obvious, but all too often I hear consultants describe customers who they think could use their services but are unclear about how important the issue or need is or who have the need but it isn't pressing (i.e., this is a concern, but not the one keeping them up all night). In other words, the demand may not be enough to drive potential customers to listen to your pitch, review a proposal, work you into their budget, or take the other steps needed to hire you.

Second, they have the responsibility to make a decision to hire you. I will talk much more about this in the section titled "Get Customers," but for now, know that the shorter the path to sale, the better. Meaning, the fewer steps it takes to move from your first conversation to signing a deal, the better. The shorter pathway means that the deal is less likely to fall apart along the way, or take such an investment in selling the project that it is no longer cost effective, even if you win. Accordingly, you are much better served, with your limited sales and marketing resources, to work with those who can make the decision to hire you, rather than those who will need you to make a presentation to their boss (and then their boss's boss) to get your project approved.

Third, even with responsibility, if they lack resources (i.e., financial means) to engage you, they aren't viable customers. This is not being callous but realistic. Anyone who is a part of the nonprofit world—whether you are in a nonprofit or serving them—is doing the work in large part out of a sense of mission, not for the money. At the same time, if you can't generate a profit, you won't be able to help anyone for long. And if you are out of business, you're having no social impact at all. If you want to change the world, you have to keep your organization going, which means bringing in the revenue to cover costs and build for your future (i.e., profit).

I have a final thought on defining your market. I highly recommend that you focus on where you are generating value right now. That is, don't make this exercise about where you want to be five or ten years from now. I will talk about the latter in the last section titled "Get Growing." For now, you need to focus on the first sales that build profitability and momentum. I see the tension of the "here and now" versus the "aspirational" customer in particular with foundation markets. Many consultants perceive national foundations as providing a level of prestige and funding that is attractive (and it is), so that is where they want to start marketing. However, right here and now, they are usually focused on smaller local or regional foundations. It may not be as well funded or prestigious, but if they are your market right now, embrace them.

EXERCISE THREE: DEFINING YOUR NICHE

Find a time and place that will allow you to concentrate. Give yourself an hour to work.

- **Step One: How Big Is Your Room?**—Does it hold fifty people? One hundred? Ten thousand? The easiest way to hone in on this is to think about how large a project you will need (based on past experience or your own estimate). The larger the project size, the fewer number of clients you will need. The converse is also true. If you are going to undertake smaller projects, you'll most likely need a larger pool of potential clients (i.e., you are selling volume).

- **Step Two: Who Is Your Client?**—For people who have seen value in your work already, ask yourself:
  - What kind of organization are they in? Is it large or small?
  - What services do they provide and to whom?
  - How long have they been in the field?
  - Where do they sit in the organization?
  - Are they primarily in one geographic location?
  - What are their pressing needs?
  - Are their preconditions ahead of their seeing value? Do they need to know something or have experienced something before they can understand your value?

- **Step Three: Can They Fit?**—When you answered the questions in step two, were you left with a number of potential clients who can fit in your room? Are there too many or too few? You may not know the exact number of potential clients out there, but use your best guess, or pull a number if possible.

  For example, if you are selling to foundation executive directors and CEOs in the Southeast region of the United States, you can research that number. If there are too few to fit in your room, look at how you have constrained the number. Is there a way to broaden your audience? If too many, look at ways to reduce, especially by geography. As I will discuss later, your personal relationships are crucial to sales and marketing—do they extend across the nation, or are they really only in two or three states?

Some of you may wonder about what you do if you have more than one niche. If you are starting up, I recommend starting with one niche—there's going to be a lot to do, so a single niche can be the sole focus of what resources (not only money but time) you have. If you are an established firm, run this exercise multiple times, but also ask yourself if every niche is needed and viable. We started honing in on a niche because when we defined our market too broadly, it became overwhelming. The same could be true if you have too many niches you are trying to serve. It may feel like you are focused, but with too many niches, you are creating the same challenge of having too large a market.

YOUR SERVICES AND PRODUCTS

In your client conversations about value, you would've heard a great deal about the services and products that make you valuable. For example, a client recently told me that Civitas Strategies gave her organization a clear path to growth (our value). I did that through a service (strategic planning) that resulted in a product (the strategic plan).

For most of you, your services and products will be clear. But for some, they may not be, or they may seem like too many to list (e.g., you are doing many small tasks as part of a larger support effort).

In cases such as these, list the activities that had value for a client, and see if there is an overarching theme or title that could cover them and be billed as a flexible service. For example, you may be adept at designing and implementing both implementation and outcome evaluations. Though they are very different, you may still boil them down to providing an evaluation service.

If you still can't categorize your service or product, this is another opportunity to engage some critical friends in helping you think it through. Meet with two or three critical friends, and lay out your services and products. Better yet, have them written down, and share them ahead of time—even if it is just a bulleted list. When you meet, ask them how you can cut the list in half by grouping, then in half again, and so on until the list is shorter and more clear. Most of the time you'll find the process moving very quickly. A friend with perspective can see the forest for the trees and pick out the themes in a short time.

As an example of this process, let me share the birth of Civitas Strategies's advisement service. In 2013, I started to engage more clients who needed a variety of services.

I was working primarily with nonprofit CEOs, and coaching was a core part of the service. But there was more than that, including some services that were ongoing and others that were more occasional. Our clients raved about the value we were producing, but every time I tried to talk about it, I struggled with a term. When meeting with a colleague, I laid out all the services it entailed, including

- providing coaching, not only for the CEO but also for the senior and midlevel managers, as needed, to ensure alignment;
- providing thought partnership on not only strategy but also the day-to-day challenges that arise in running an organization that you can't take to your board or to your staff; and
- being as-needed staff by reviewing communications, creating specialized documents for high-profile funding opportunities, or just performing tasks that were beyond staff capacity.

It was definitely a team service, provided not just by myself but also by my associates.

After laying all this out, the colleague quickly noticed that what Civitas Strategies offered was different and she hadn't heard of other firms doing it. She referred to it as an advisory role, which later evolved into the term "advisement." For the first time, I had a word to bundle all the services and products into as well as a way to describe it. (I call it the CEO's Swiss Army knife.) Since then, advisement has been our greatest seller.

When you are pulling your services together, I'd like to make two important points. First, limit them in number, especially if you are just starting out. I use the range of five to seven a lot (the number of things you can keep in ready memory in your head), but for services, think one to four. That's right, even one service or product alone is fine if there is a strong enough market. I suggest this because starting up or even just running your small consultancy is challenging enough—having to build multiple products and services can be overwhelming. The focus on a limited number of products and services also allows you to put your energy into gaining momentum. As I will talk about later in section two ("Get Customers"), your best prospects are people who already engaged you (those who re-up) or send a colleague to you (those who refer). Accordingly, the faster you start to build a client base in one service or product, the more likely you are to hit a critical mass of re-ups and referrals that will further accelerate your business.

Second, for every service you must have a success story ready. It is perfectly fine if you are starting out and the success story is from when you were working elsewhere. You want to be able to relate the story quickly—I suggest a three-part format. The first sentence tells what the situation was when you arrived (e.g., "growth was stalled for five years"); second, what you did (e.g., "we facilitated a simple five-step planning process with the board, staff, and key stakeholders focused on the biggest challenge"); and third, the outcome (e.g., "the resulting plan created two new strategic partnerships that provided the resources for growth").

ON PURPOSE

You can make a living in consulting for nonprofits, but it is also likely that it is about more than just a paycheck. Without fail, everyone I have met who is in this field is concurrently driven by a desire to help people. It's important, for the design of your organization and how you communicate your consultancy to others, to be clear on your purpose. Put simply, I am asking, "What is it that you are trying to accomplish?" You want your purpose to reflect your passion as well as your profession.

You may ask, isn't that a mission or a vision? Yes and no. It includes elements of each but is also distinct. More importantly, I find when you talk "mission" and "vision," people start to worry about format and the "rules" of creating it. For example, does your mission have to start with "to..."

About ten years ago, I was at a planning session with a client who actually used an entire two-hour planning session to determine just the structure (not the content) of the organization's mission and vision. Since that meeting, I've avoided using those terms and instead use "purpose" or "aspiration" to help clients focus on what they want to say rather than the rules about how to say it.

EXERCISE FOUR: FINDING YOUR PURPOSE

Find a quiet place where you can have about an hour to yourself.

- **Step One: Review Everything You've Done Until Now**—Look at your value, niche, and services, and think about how you are contributing to the world.
- **Step Two: Find What You Want to Achieve**—Forget for a moment that you are a for-profit, a nonprofit, or just a person in an office and ask yourself the following questions:
  - What do you want to do that transcends your organizational structure?
  - What is it that you want to do to impact the world?
  - If you spend the rest of your professional life on this endeavor, what do you want to be able to show for it?

  Write down the answers to your questions.
- **Step Three: Distillation**—Now take what you have written, and try to distill it down to one sentence or idea. This will take a few tries. If you have a lot of text, try to cut the number of words in half, then cut it by another half, and so on, until you have one sentence. Make sure it is a tight sentence. This is an exercise in essence and simplicity, not how many clauses you can work into one sentence!

Now take this sentence out into the world, and test it. Try it with at least ten of your critical friends—those you trust and who will be honest with you. Refine it each time based on their feedback, but at the same time, keep the language tight. Your purpose should be short and sweet, but at the same time, it should reflect both the work you do as a consultant and the way that you want to help change the world.

Finally, give it one last test. Ask yourself if you are inspired by it. This is your enterprise, your vehicle for helping the world—is your passion and vision being conveyed? If you aren't inspired by it, you are not going to go far. Ensure that you make this the last ultimate test of your purpose—ensure that it is what you want to fulfill.

When I work with consultants, this is often a difficult moment. They do have a passion for the work, but at the same time, they feel self-conscious because they're doing it through a for-profit enterprise. This is all true; you are working as a for-profit or at least in your own self-interest to some degree, but you are also contributing to the public good. It is crucial that you recognize that.

This exercise can lead to a very important shift in not only how you describe your business but also how you perceive it yourself. For the first few years of Civitas Strategies, I described us as management consultancy supporting nonprofit organizations. This was true but, at the same time, unsatisfactory since all of us were driven by a larger vision of contributing to the world. I realized, however, that these do not need to be mutually exclusive. Our purpose is to better the lives of families and children, but I also recognize that we do so by improving the effectiveness of the organizations we serve. Those organizations, our clients, do the hard work, but at the same time, we make a contribution too.

SIZING UP THE COMPETITION

Knowing your competition is crucial, but know from the outset that when I talk about competition, I'm not just referring to other firms that are providing the same or similar services. I want you to think about your competition more broadly to include the following:

- **Direct Competition**—This includes both nonprofit and for-profit companies in your niche that are offering the same or similar services.
- **Substitutes**—This refers to other solutions that companies may be using instead of engaging you or anyone to provide certain services or products.

For example, if you offer a curriculum, they may be able to have staff cobble one together themselves.

- **Inaction**—Over and over again, I will mention that nonprofits don't have much or any excess funds, and this has an outsized impact on their behavior (and in turn the market you're working in). As a result, many times, if there isn't a policy mandate, an emergency, or financial urgency, nonprofit leaders will opt to delay or forgo engaging outside firms, even though it would be beneficial in the long run.

Accordingly, it is crucial to know why they "must" (if at all) engage your organization for your services and products. This doesn't mean that you drop your endeavor if there isn't a mandate, but rather be aware that the impact of your services may not outweigh budgetary constraints and fiscal conservatism.

EXERCISE FIVE: COMPETITOR ANALYSIS

Competitor analyses are a bit like an accordion—they can be small and tight or wide and far reaching. I've done both types and find that for most nonprofit consultancies, a smaller, focused competitor analysis will be more helpful. For the exercise, you'll need about eight hours in total, most likely not in one sitting. Much of it doesn't need to be done by you, so consider outsourcing or delegating parts to maximize your time.

- **Step One: Pull Your Interview Data**—Start with the notes from your conversations. There were a number of questions on who provides the same or similar services (and likely if potential clients are choosing inaction, the interview questions will reveal it). List the relevant points from each interview, and then group them by similar theme or idea. Next, consolidate them as much as possible to keep the set of ideas as manageable as possible. There's no hard-and-fast number you're trying to consolidate to, but the tighter, the better.
- **Step Two: Collect Data on the Competition**—Search Google and LinkedIn to find potential competitors in your niche. This is emphasized to remind you that there will always be competitors somewhere in the world. The key issue is whether they are sharing a market niche with you—not just offering the same services or products but offering them to your potential customers.

    Over the years, I have found that if you can identify ten to twenty competitors, you will have enough grist for your analysis. Will there be others you missed? Maybe, but these will be the most significant (since they were the easiest to find). Record their names, websites (so you can go back easily if needed), services they offer, how they describe their niche, and any apparent differences or advantages they have in relation to your offerings.

    Create a grid where the "y" axis (the leftmost column) lists your key services and products and the "x" axis (the topmost row) contains the categories of completion I mentioned previously (i.e., competitor offerings, substitutes, and inaction). Now add in your observations on the market into each cell in the grid.
- **Step Three: Analyze the Results**—Write down the answers to these questions:
    - Where is competition the least?
    - Where is it the greatest?

○ What factors and with whom are you competing? Is it price? (e.g., the option most people choose for that service is inaction; they will probably be very price sensitive to a service that they believe they can defer).

○ If you are competing with other firms, what are their characteristics? How are you different or the same?

As you assess the competitive landscape, look for the tangible and intangible. For example, customers may choose your competitor because of a clear, tangible factor, such as your competitor has a better, easier-to-use website, can bundle multiple services together for cost-effectiveness, or is based in the same geographic location. Also be on the lookout for intangible factors, such as relationships or perceived expertise. These intangibles are often just as crucial but are much more difficult to mitigate.

Let's run through a quick example of a competitor analysis with a lighter subject: the rare date night. A few months ago, my wife and I secured a babysitter and were planning a night out. We always enjoy our trip to Cambridge, Massachusetts, which is known for its restaurants and shops, and the energy around the city. Our first choice is usually Harvest, a wonderful local restaurant that provides gourmet food using primarily local ingredients. However, there are other restaurants that we enjoy going to as well. Those are our options.

Service	Competitor Offering	Substitutions	Inaction
Harvest Restaurant (local sourced)	• Rialto (Italian) • Oleana (Mediterranean) • Craigie on Main (French)	• Get the boys out of the house and make an upscale meal myself • Go outside the city	Have dinner with the boys, per usual *Stressed out parents!*

We could also opt to not go to Cambridge and go to a restaurant in a different town. We could also try to drop the boys off at the babysitter's house and make a fancy meal at home (I'm not too bad a cook).

And, of course, there's always the option of not doing anything at all. Then our kids are going to have to deal with some stressed-out parents with no quality time together, so let's not even consider that one!

In this example, we ended up in another city that was closer, with shorter and easier travel—an example of how substitutions do happen.

YOUR BLUE OCEAN AND UNFAIR ADVANTAGE

Now that you have an idea of the competitive landscape (i.e., what is happening in the world around you), we are going to use this information to discover your unfair advantage. Your unfair advantage includes ways in which your organization, connections, services, and products are better than any of your competitors' or the alternatives that prospective customers may choose.

Let's start by talking briefly about the ideas of blue oceans and red oceans as defined in Renée Mauborgne and W. Chan Kim's *Blue Ocean Strategy*. A red ocean is a niche with a lot of competition or some particularly strong competitors. In the non-profit world, an example is large-scale outcome evaluations. Firms like the American Institutes for Research have a strong reputation and capacity that overshadows most other firms.

In contrast, a blue ocean is one where there is little competition. This could be because you are in a new or underserved niche; it could also be that it is the *way* you are serving the niche (i.e., the products and services you offer) that make it a blue ocean. For example, I believe that there is a blue ocean in apps to serve nonprofits. The nonprofit world tends to be slow to adopt and use technology and usually has older equipment. Apps running on smartphones tend to be easier to use and more accessible, providing an opportunity to unitize technology in new ways to serve nonprofit leaders.

Your blue ocean is not only a function of the competition but also a function of you and your organization and offerings. Accordingly, understanding your unfair advantage is crucial to knowing if you are in a blue ocean or how to get into one. Your unfair advantage is a differentiator from your competition or the alternative solutions to your clients' needs that provide you with outsized competitive advantage.

That was a mouthful! What does it mean? Put simply, your unfair advantage is what you do better than the competition. Just like we did during the competitor analysis, you need to consider the tangible and intangible. An example of a tangible unfair advantage is a client who, a few years ago, developed a framework and approach to child development that relied on cutting-edge research that had never been bridged to the classroom. Education leaders recognized the unique nature of the product, the need for the product, and that there was nothing comparable and began to rapidly adopt it.

As for an intangible, I often look at a client's relationships. A past client was transitioning from working at a philanthropic foundation to the consulting world. She was concerned because she knew a lot of people in the foundation world but few beyond it. I suggested this was her unfair advantage—that these relationships gave her a connection and understanding of philanthropy that few consultants had, therefore increasing her ability to help foundation leaders.

Here are some other examples of unfair advantages of our clients (of course, adjusted for confidentiality):

- Deep experience guiding educational leaders of some of the largest urban school districts in the United States
- The ability to listen to clients and see opportunities that others miss
- Having "big city" consulting experience and now living in a rural area in which no competitors have your talents and skills

Remember, your unfair advantage is not static—as the market changes, you may need to adjust as well. In the first example I mentioned, other organizations, seeing the demand for the unique product, began to create similar ones and suddenly the blue ocean started to turn red. In reaction, our client needed to offer additional, related products to get back ahead of her competition.

EXERCISE SIX: FINDING YOUR UNFAIR ADVANTAGE

This is one of the most difficult exercises in this book because about 90 percent of the time, the consultants I have worked with miss the forest for the trees and gravitate to what they think their unfair advantage is versus what their interviewees told them. Accordingly, if you are doing this yourself, allow for a great deal of time thinking about the data and results—at least one if not two hours. Better yet, engage a critical friend in the process. Ideally, if you know the right person, you should share the information from your competitor analysis and your answers to the questions in steps two and three, so he or she can independently "test" your assumptions and results. Alternatively, invite your critical friend to do the exercise with you to act as a real-time foil for your thinking.

- **Step One:** Review all your interview notes from exercise two and your analysis from exercise four. Take note of what it says about your value. Compare the results with the strengths of your competitors as identified in exercise five.
- **Step Two:** Answer the following questions:
  - What do you do or have that is better than the competition? Consider both tangible and intangible assets. If there is more than one, can they be grouped or reduced? You want to get to the clearest point or points possible.
  - How can you describe this advantage to others? Go beyond just stating it by identifying how it provides a "pain or gain" for customers (i.e., mitigate a problem they face or help advance their work).
  - What is the next level for your unfair advantage? How can you strengthen it further or anticipate competitors? This could be through the development of new or related services and products, training, talent acquisition (i.e., bringing on people with complementary skills), networking, or other activities.
- **Step Three:** Adjust your definition of your value, niche, and products and services to ensure you are in the bluest ocean possible. Ask yourself the following questions:
  - How can I define my value to distinguish myself from my competition?
  - If I shift, who is "in the room" of my niche? Can I change the number of competitors?

○   What products and services alone or in combination are least represented in the market?

○   Is your pricing in line with your competitors?

Remember, blue oceans can become red oceans over time, so I strongly recommend revisiting this exercise at least once a year.

GETTING TO KNOW YOU

The final activity in this chapter is taking what you've accomplished so far and putting it all on one page—it shouldn't be longer than that and will most likely be much shorter. This one page is your charter and will immediately give you a guide for not only creating your business but also engaging others along the way. I'm often asked, "Who is the audience for the charter?" First and foremost, it is you—this is your go-to document for articulating what you are trying to do. I will build on it later to create your control panel, but for now this is your go-to document for answering the question, "What are you doing?"

Your charter is something that you don't need to commit to memory immediately—you'll do that in time. In the meantime, be gentle with yourself, and keep it handy—on paper and electronically in multiple places so you can access it easily. If you're on a phone call, keep it handy, and don't hesitate to use it for talking points. What is important right now is that you start to use your charter as a guide and concurrently test its ability to communicate your work effectively. To that last point, this means the charter is a living document that will be updated and honed as you receive feedback. Even now, I update our Civitas Strategies charter almost every sixty to ninety days based on feedback. The edits are not huge shifts, but rather mostly small changes in words that better convey our value.

2

Creating the MVC—Structure

In this section we're going to focus on creating the minimum viable company (MVC)—an approach to rapidly starting an organization that allows you to quickly move from your vision to a profitable business that can grow over time. I'm going to start with the basics: naming your organization and establishing a legal entity. I will also talk about how to convert your legal entity. If you are already an existing consultancy, you will still want to review this section to ensure you have the best structure for your work.

I'll then move to the next chapter, which completes the MVC, helping you create your robot office, which automates many of your core operations using a suite of low-/no-cost technologies that will give you large office support on a small business budget.

The MVC is an outcropping of the lean-thinking movement, which is a useful way of thinking for your company development and your work with clients. Lean thinking has evolved greatly since it was first described by Eric Ries in his book, *The Lean Startup*, which marked a shift in the technology start-ups. The basic idea is that too many companies wait until they have everything figured out before moving into the market (from their basic vision through creating and testing each service and product). The result is that these companies are so slow to market, especially in the fast-paced world of technology, that at times entire opportunities are missed. This old, intensive approach also requires a large start-up cost, since so much effort is made before you ever have a sale, thus creating a barrier for many entrepreneurs to create their companies.

The Lean Startup diverges from the traditional approach and instead emphasizes moving to market while you cast your products and services with your potential customers. First and foremost, it is about creating a minimum viable product: take the minimum product that you have, and start talking to your customers about it to get their feedback. This could be as simple as a cardboard model or a full prototype. Once you have this minimum viable product, you're constantly testing it and evolving it over time with your customers. To be clear, lean is not a free-for-all. It also includes using key performance indicators to measure your success and keep you on track. The result is what is termed the build-measure-learn cycle, where you iteratively build prototypes, measure their success, learn from the results, refine your product and services, and shape them into another prototype to test. Though the lean movement is very much geared toward technology and products, I have found it to be a crucial framework not only for starting up and growing consultancies but also in working with our nonprofit clients who are often in extremely resource-constrained environments, creating an opportunity to focus on small tests to make progress and attract new funding rather than waiting for the development of (and funding needed for) entirely new services.

CASH FLOW BY DESIGN

When developing your MVC, I also want you to keep cash flow in mind. In advising clients, I always suggest that cash flow is your number-two concern behind profitability. Most basically, cash flow is how money comes in and out of your business. At the most basic level, if you're not earning enough, then you won't have the cash coming in to pay yourself and your expenses, leading to a rapid end to your venture. However, this is not usually the most significant manifestation of cash-flow issues. When income is lean, people are usually aware of it and cut back and work diligently to manage their cash flow.

The bigger issue is when you don't have a sales problem. In cases like this, entrepreneurs often become complacent, saying to themselves, "I have more than enough business to pay our expenses and make a profit." What's tricky about cash flow is that even if you have enough work, if the money doesn't flow in at the same time as it's flowing out, you can end up in a cash crunch that could make your life stressful or even end your business. Accordingly, throughout the design and operation of your business, you should be thinking about how fast money will flow in and how fast it will flow out. For example, when you structure a contract, include an up-front payment to provide yourself with a reserve of cash as you begin executing your project, rather than waiting until you've done a significant amount of work to receive some payment. It can even affect how you spend your time, day by day, minute by minute. When all tasks are equal, I always recommend undertaking the project that will allow you to draw cash quickly, because once you have the cash, it is there to spend and mitigates cash-flow risk.

YOUR NEW BEST FRIEND: TASK MANAGEMENT

"Are you really about to discuss task management? That's so tactical!" I've heard that too many times to mention from nonprofit consultants. And, yes, I'm going to delve into task management for two reasons. First, chances are that if you're reading this book, you are a professional who has had some degree of support staff. That might mean an administrative assistant or subordinates, and probably that also means staff outside of your direct reports, such as information-technology support staff, a finance team, and others who would handle a lot of different operational tasks for you on your behalf. Often, these staff probably addressed tasks without your knowledge. In the typical nonprofit consultancy, you are it—from start-up to execution, or close to it. Accordingly, there are many, many tasks for you to manage, and failing on any can hurt your client relationships and business.

Second, being timely is a key differentiator for your consultancy. At least once a month, a client comments that one of Civitas Strategies's key differences from other consultancies is that we deliver on time. It is amazing to me that most nonprofit consultancies do not. A solid task-management system keeps you on track to complete your projects on time and also distinguish your firm as one of the few who can!

With this in mind, one of the first things I recommend to clients, whether they are just starting out or have consulted for years, is to make sure they have a strong task-management system. A solid task-management system includes a software component but more importantly a method for how you are going to intake, prioritize, and address your tasks.

FINDING YOUR SYSTEM

I should confess that I am one of those people who enjoys learning about and testing task-management systems, whether it's a new app or a new approach. There are a lot of systems out there that are very good. I particularly recommend Stephen Covey's *Seven Habits of Highly Effective People* and David Allen's *Getting Things Done*.

Drawing on many other systems I've tested over the years, I have constructed my own approach, which synthesizes the best practices of the various options. I use three components.

First, I keep Covey's four quadrants in mind for my task prioritization. Covey offers four quadrants with "x" axis parsing tasks that are urgent or not (i.e., the action is needed in the near future) and the "y" axis showing if the task is important or not. Appropriately, Covey recommends that you get the urgent/important things done all the time—you have to. On the opposite end, anything that is not urgent and is unimportant should be sloughed off—these tasks are not that critical. The key focus should then be on the important but not urgent tasks—these are the ones that can eventually become urgent too late. The classic example of this in consultancies is sales and marketing—you focus on the urgent and important client's work and delay on developing your pipeline. However, when all your projects end, the pipeline becomes very important and urgent!

Second, I organize all my tasks by project—both personal and professional—in the same system. David Allen, author of *Getting Things Done*, converted me over to mixing both work and personal to dos with the reasoning that you cannot bifurcate your personal life and your professional life—they are part of the same life. And this is especially true for the consultant who is actively engaging in lifestyle integration—you want to be able to fluidly prioritize the work and the personal side of your life as needed.

Third, I prioritize my list overall, assigning tasks to days of the week and also breaking down my schedule for each day. I start my day with everything that can be done quickly, usually under five minutes. This allows me to get some items quickly checked off. After that, I proceed based on importance to speed up the inflow of cash, client service, sustain the organization, and everything else (in that order). When thinking about your day, consider your natural tendencies and the tasks you have to accomplish. For example, I'm most effective when I write before noon, so when a writing assignment is pending, I will put off calls until the afternoon so I can have my morning to focus. Alternatively, I'm almost always up for telephone calls, so I work them into my day whenever they fit. Know your personal strengths and preferences, and work them to your advantage.

As for software, there are a number of apps, web and smartphone based, that are very good and of low or no cost. I have used Wunderlist and find it the best currently available. However, there are always new products appearing. (Check the smallbut-mightybook.com website for reviews and updates.) Look for tools that allow you to not only do everything listed here (prioritize tasks and assign them to projects) but also share them with and delegate them to others. Even if you aren't working with any-one else right now, you may want the ability to start collaborating using a task system in the future, so I recommend ensuring you have the capacity up front.

A ROSE BY ANY OTHER NAME

Whether you are just starting out or have been consulting for years, the name of your venture is a key component and one you want to set early. When I first started shaping my firm, I interviewed people about my value. One of the things they pointed out was that I had my own style of consulting that was very valuable and that, for all intents and purposes, I was the brand. So when I opened my doors on the first day of the year in 2010, I did so as Romano Consulting. After two years, I decided to incorporate (I will talk more about that later in the book). As I was preparing to do so, a key client suggested that I do so under a different name. This was the dialogue:

Client: The problem with Romano Consulting is that it sounds like it is just a guy at a desk in his house.

Me: But that's what I am.

Client: We both know that, but finance departments ask a lot more ques-tions about businesses that they think are tiny than those that they think are larger. If you have a company name, they will stop asking so many questions because you won't sound like a guy at a desk in his house.

And so the name Civitas Strategies was born.

This was a very important lesson for me and opened my eyes to the need for branding outside of just my name. In retrospect, it created a significant differentiator for me. Both clients who knew me and new clients I met noted that the name change alone gave them the sense that the company was a larger, more mature firm than others—even ones that had been in existence far longer but used the name of the principal. For example, as Romano Consulting I had a few questions from potential clients about my capacity to execute projects alone. Since I changed the name to Civitas Strategies, there's never been a question about our size or capacity. The new name also associated me with the more established firms in the field (such as The Bridgespan Group) rather than the greater preponderance of nonprofit consultants who just use their names (such as J. P. Smith Associates).

I suggest setting a name as soon as possible for your venture. If you are in a start-up, the name gives you something to reference in your conversations. For example, it is a lot easier and more engaging to say, "I'm currently starting up a consultancy called Civitas Strategies," than, "I'm working on creating a consultancy." The former sounds like you have a plan; the latter could be seen as being unsure. For a new or existing consultancy, having a name also formalizes the venture in your mind and those of potential clients. Don't underestimate the effect this will have on your confidence and excitement in your consultancy and the effect this will have on the image that prospective clients have of your company. You will be seen as more solid and formal, not a temporary venture.

As you consider names, avoid using your own name at all costs—even in some permutation that implies a larger organization (like Romano Associates or Romano Consulting Group). A company name that is detached from the principal tends be more effective at conveying that you are a large organization. That is not to discourage you from being a consultancy, but it just reflects the need to have client's confidence and trust, which tends to be built much more quickly with the impression of a larger operation.

Beyond choosing a name that is not tied to an individual, select a name that has meaning to you and your market niche. Also consider having some fun with it. In the 1990s, I founded a small public-relations and communications consultancy with two partners. We chose the name Snake Oil Consulting, a mercurial reflection on the profession, which is often about how you communicate over what it is that you're communicating about. The name always got a smile, started conversations, and was rarely forgotten.

In deciding the name for Civitas Strategies, I wanted to choose one that conveyed the public-service aspect of our work, that we are serving not just nonprofit organizations but any organization, for-profit and nonprofit, that serves the public good. I also wanted to tie it to our core value—strategy design and execution. Finally, I am an ancient history geek, and so choosing a Latin word for the community at large had personal resonance. Hence, Civitas Strategies was born.

EXERCISE SEVEN: DISCOVERING THE NAME

I purposely write "discovering" your name because I suspect most of you already have it in your subconscious and need to bring it to the surface. This exercise will require some short bursts over two or three weeks. (Do not go longer than three weeks, and try to keep it to two; otherwise, you are likely to keep churning and not making a decision and moving to the next step.) Though none of the activities are time consuming, make sure that when you are brainstorming in step one, you do so in a quiet place where you won't be interrupted.

For those of you in established firms, you can use this same process to move away from a "named" company (like I did moving from Romano Consulting to Civitas Strategies) or just coming up with a new name for your venture.

- **Step One: Brainstorm**—Start by listing no more than five things you want the name to convey. Include points on the following:
  - your core business or service (e.g., "strategies" in Civitas Strategies)
  - a differentiator (e.g., my friend and colleague Khaatim Sheerer El named his firm "ResultsDriven" based on his commitment to results over process)
  - something fun or something about you personally (e.g., the "Snake Oil" or "Civitas" examples I mentioned previously)

  Generate keywords based on your list. It is helpful to use a table in Microsoft Word or a spreadsheet in Microsoft Excel so you can easily make combinations. Generate one- or two-word company names based on your keywords (once you have three words, people tend to want to replace them with an acronym).

  Keep an Internet-connected device handy so you can search for potential name conflicts. Include searches on your state database of existing and former businesses so you can see what is already taken. You should also search the Internet to find other organizations nationally using the name or acronym if you are using one.

- **Step Two: Test and Refine**—When you are down to five or fewer possibilities, test them with at least ten critical friends. Your venture will last you years, so you want to make sure it is something that not only you can live with but also others will be able to understand and be comfortable using. You want to ask them if the name is

- similar or the same as other firms they know of;
- descriptive of you and the value you generate; and
- easily pronounced and remembered.

It is highly likely that this will generate some revisions. Once you have it down to a selection you like, start using it with others for at least three weeks before committing to test the response and your comfort with it.

Remember that, ultimately, this name is yours, so make sure it is one you want to live with every day for years. When in doubt, go with the name that resonates most with you.

TO INCORPORATE OR NOT TO INCORPORATE

Let me start with a caveat that covers the entire section on incorporation—I'm not a lawyer, and the information I am going to provide should not be construed as legal advice. I strongly recommend that as you create your company, you seek the help of a qualified attorney. As I'll explain in a moment, I did not start out as a corporation. When I did incorporate, I did not seek legal advice, opting to do it myself, and it was a painful lesson learned. Incorporating should be an easy process that any citizen can undertake, but unfortunately it is much more convoluted and complex than most are willing or able to navigate. Know that as I talk about corporate structure, this is a starting point for your later conversations with legal counsel to give you the lay of the land.

When I founded my consultancy in 2010, I was a mix of the Temp and the Hamster archetypes as described in the introduction. I had decided to leave the consultancy I had been working for to pursue establishing my own firm. I wasn't fully confident that I would be able to make it alone, so like the Temp, I didn't allow myself to commit fully to consulting. Like the Hamster, I was trying to do everything myself to reduce costs. Unsurprisingly, I took the least expensive, easiest route to establish my organization— I became a sole proprietorship (which essentially means I declared myself a business without incorporating). I will go into more detail about different types of businesses later, but for now, it is important to note that I created the organization based on what was most expedient, not on the best fit for the long term.

After two years of consulting, I was no longer the Temp archetype and was fully committed to the profession and building my business, so I incorporated as a limited liability corporation (LLC). The LLC would prove a much better fit for me personally and professionally. But here is where I made my second mistake—I did it myself. As I later realized, getting professional help to incorporate is not that expensive, and for the novice, the time it takes to learn and do it simultaneously is great. By the end of the process, I felt like I had spent about one hundred hours from start to finish—time taken away from my consulting with clients and bringing in revenue.

This is why I strongly recommend that you think about the structure that's going to be best for you in the long term and engage professional assistance to do it cost-effectively. And to be clear, I give this advice even to the people who are consciously consulting to fill the gap between two jobs. I find increasingly that most mid- to senior-level professionals have multiple opportunities for side consulting or consulting between positions throughout their career. Therefore, the investment and having the right organization, and maintaining it even when you're working a full-time job, can be beneficial as well.

DECISIONS, DECISIONS

Though you should seek legal counsel in establishing your company, I still want to give you some background information so that when you do talk to a lawyer, you're "smarter than the average bear." There are really three types of structures that you can have as a consultant: sole proprietorship, nonprofit corporation, or for-profit corporation (including a nonprofit, C, S, or LLC).

The easiest one to create is a sole proprietorship. Essentially, this amounts to you declaring that you are, personally, an enterprise. You are the company, and you use your own Social Security number as the identifier for the enterprise. Though there is little to do for the federal government at the start, typically your state and locality will have filing requirements—usually you can find these on your state's secretary of state or office of economic development's website. Typically, you can also use a business name separate from your own by registering your "doing business as" (DBA) name in accordance with state and local laws. At tax time, all the profits and losses go to your personal taxes using some additional forms.

The sole proprietorship is a quick, easy, and inexpensive route, but there are disadvantages. You will need to pay self-employment tax, which can be higher than the combined employee and company contributions to taxes for a corporation. You also tend to have a greater legal liability as a sole proprietorship if something goes catastrophically wrong.

If you forgo being a sole proprietorship, your remaining options are incorporation. Most basically, incorporation means that you're creating a separate "corpus" or body—a legal entity that is separate from yourself.

The first question before incorporating that you need to answer is for-profit or nonprofit? Most consultants don't even consider this question. They assume that if they are working to create a money-making enterprise, that means it has to be for-profit. However, this is not the case, as many nonprofits essentially function as consultancies (though, as I will discuss, there are specific requirements and constraints involved).

For many of you, being a for-profit corporation will provide greater flexibility, but concurrently, take time to consider a nonprofit corporation when one of two circumstances exist. First, when you developed your must-haves, your list may have included a mission of service. To be clear, you can have a public-service mission without being a nonprofit (e.g., at Civitas Strategies, we give 15 percent of our net profit in donations and pro-bono work). However, you may want more than that—for every excess dollar you take in, you may want it to go to other nonprofits. For example, Third Sector New England has many of the services and products of a consultancy, but all the net profits support its mission of public service.

Second, a nonprofit may also provide greater opportunity to serve your niche. A number of government and nonprofit funders, for example, have much greater flexibility in engaging nonprofit organizations over for-profits. Accordingly, by having a nonprofit organization, you may be eligible for additional funding or be more likely to secure projects.

However, being a nonprofit is not without disadvantages. At the most basic level, a nonprofit is a public-service organization with a board—that is, it is not owned by an individual. Even if you, as the founder, sit on a small board with other people you know, ultimately governance is shared. Also, you cannot take net profits out of the nonprofit. They need to be reinvested in your service or used as a limited reserve. There are also additional reporting and legal requirements that generally make them less nimble than for-profits.

For most of you, a for-profit corporation will be a better fit. There are four corporation types you will most likely consider: C corporations, S corporations, LLCs, and partnerships. Let's take a closer look at each.

Most of the large companies you see and hear about are C corporations. The C corporation is owned by shareholders. The structure is easier for large enterprises since it allows ownership to be transferred through shares. They are also the most complex in terms of their legal requirements and the most expensive to run in terms of administrative fees and taxes. I can imagine few scenarios where the structure will be appealing for consultants, especially running small- or midsized firms.

In reaction to the complexities of owning a C corporation, the federal government created a small-business version, called an S corporation. The S corporation is a separate legal entity from you personally (like a C corporation) but is limited in the number of owners. Any profit you take out of an S corporation flows into your personal taxes, so it is usually a less complex structure to manage throughout the year and at tax time. The structure also means that the corporation itself is not receiving profits (they flow to your personal taxes); therefore, you typically are not subject to corporate taxation.

LLCs usually offer small business owners the greatest ease at start-up, flexibility, and ownership. LLCs can be owned by one or more individuals and are governed first and foremost by your state. For LLCs, the federal government lets you decide how you want your company to be treated for tax purposes (e.g., as a S or C corporation). That election can change over time, so you can adjust as your business grows. They also tend to be less expensive to establish than other corporations. Civitas Strategies is an LLC that elects to be treated as an S corporation.

A partnership is a business where two or more individuals share ownership. Each person contributes equally in terms of the investments of the business but also shares the profits and losses of the organization in the same way. Because of the nature of the partnership being shared governance, typically there are very explicit processes to address how to resolve disputes, share profits, and change ownership. Partnerships are usually inexpensive to set up, but they also have shared liability and governance to a degree that will probably be unattractive to consultants.

3

Creating the MVC—The Robot Office

In chapter 2, I created the structure for your MVC. Now I will set up the infrastructure. It has never been easier to run a cost-effective consultancy. The game changer is the rapid growth of technology that can help you have big company infrastructure at a small company cost. These technologies are not only more numerous than ever before, they are also smarter and more cost effective. Taken together, I affectionately refer to this as the "robot office"—the suite of apps, cloud-based services, telephony, and software that almost instantly create a company without additional people.

Over the years I've found most consultants and aspiring consultants in the non-profit world are usually unfamiliar with existing technologies and often uncomfortable with them. But returning to one of our earlier concepts, profitability, the robot office is crucial to your success. Accordingly, particularly if you are technophobic, this is a time where you may need to force yourself to grow for the sake of your company and your dreams.

The robot office has five elements, each of which is described herein.

ELEMENT ONE: SPACE TO WORK

When it comes to space, in the interest of profitability, I usually recommend not renting commercial space, but instead using your home. Even then, you will want to designate a work area. Some of you will immediately respond that there isn't space in your home or that it might not be conducive to working (e.g., your children may be at home full time and a constant distraction). In cases like this, I would strongly encourage you to find a space that can work for you—and that is cost-free. Increasingly, people are working from cafés, libraries, and other public spaces. This may not work for everyone, but if it can work for you, I would strongly suggest it since it keeps your costs low.

Also, know that you don't have to use the same space all the time. When it comes to technology, I strongly recommend consultants get a laptop or a tablet they're comfortable using—even if they're working from home and an office. You just never know when you might want a change of pace—or want to take the opportunity to work outside and enjoy a sunny day. Having technology that allows you to easily move frees you from the constraint of space and gives you many more options.

I gave up on an office on the arrival of our second child. At first I was nervous about not having a dedicated space, but I've actually grown to love it! Each day I can work in a different place, inside or outside of the house, and not feel like I'm tied to a chair. However, you may be in a situation where you need to have an office or physical space of some kind. If this is the case, think very strongly about your minimum space requirements. For example, maybe you need space to occasionally meet with clients. Think about whether you need that space full time or whether you could use a shared space, coworking space, or even pay an existing company for use of a conference room as needed. If you still believe that you need an office to work, ask yourself what the most stripped-down office is that you can use. The reality is, unless your clients are in that space on a constant basis, they won't see the direct value from it. So the less expensive it can be for them, the more viable and sustainable your business will be overall.

ELEMENT TWO: A BOOKKEEPING AND ACCOUNTING SYSTEM

Your bookkeeping and accounting system allows you to easily collect and track revenues and expenses as well as quickly invoice to keep the cash you need flowing in.

During the first few years of Civitas Strategies, I did all of our financial functions personally; I even took care of our tax preparation. This approach was not so much about cost cutting as it was a control issue—I knew the importance of understanding my financials intimately, and I had trouble envisioning how I could keep the awareness I wanted without having my hands in the system. Enabling my control issues was technology—managing my own system required far less time than you would imagine. However, as I have added an accountant and bookkeeper, I have found that there is a real value to having human expertise to complement the right robotic system. I learned from my mistake and created a blended financial system.

At the heart of your blended financial system will be accounting software—this is your system to capture all your revenues and expenses and is also used typically for invoicing. This sounds like it can be very complicated and time consuming, but accounting software has become very user-friendly and typically can link to most banks and credit cards to automatically do the data entry for you. A critical component is the invoicing system. Remember what I said about cash flow—it's a critical part of running your business. If you run out of cash, even if you have a lot of contracts, your business can quickly implode. Again, most of the accounting software you'll find handles invoicing in a very easy way. The bigger issue is to habituate invoicing. Most of my projects are invoiced on a monthly basis. Whenever possible I set up automatic invoicing so that if the contract says, for example, "invoice on the first day of the month," I need not worry. The system will automatically shoot out the invoice.

In terms of specific systems, I currently use QuickBooks, but I also have used FreshBooks in the past. The former was a concession to my accountant since this is really the industry standard in the field. However, FreshBooks is a great alternative that is built specifically for small businesses and that also integrates timekeeping, so that would knock off one more system for you. The other side of the accounting equation is the human element. At the very least, you're going to want an accountant who understands small businesses. The person will help you answer key questions related to how you record your expenses and revenues and address taxes (including preparing them). You may also want a bookkeeper, primarily to keep the accounting system "clean." Each month the person will look at the entries and ensure that everything is in the system in the right way so that the accountant can focus on high-level issues rather than fixing small entries. The systems can be accessed remotely; so much of this happens without you having to meet or even talk by phone.

If you are interested in finding an accountant, seek references from small business owners you know. Though your accountant can be located anywhere, make sure he or she is familiar with your state laws and regulations, so you may want to limit your search to your state. Most accounting firms also offer bookkeeping services, but they're typically much more intensive and expensive than you need. I found that the accountants I have used understand this challenge and are more than happy to refer you to bookkeepers outside of their firm who are used to dealing with even smaller businesses and will be much more cost effective.

ELEMENT THREE: TIME TRACKING

It is imperative to think of your time as rapidly expiring inventory. Think of your time as being similar to a supermarket that has apples that are constantly going bad. If they don't sell them fast enough, they won't be able to sell them at all. Additionally, going with this analogy, the more apples that go bad, the less profitable that supermarket is going to be. This is like your time—if you don't sell it, you can't get it back. And every hour that you don't sell affects your profitability. So to judge your profitability, you need to know how much time you are selling or losing. I cannot underestimate this—many times the aspiring or existing consultants I meet don't want to worry about profitability or want to do all they can for a given client. They believe their motives are noble, but in the end they're on a road to becoming the Hamster—constantly working and trying to catch up on projects because too much time was spent on other ones.

Look for a time system that's going to allow you to easily divide up your projects, assign a budget to them, and provide clear reporting on how you are doing along the way. As with your to-do system, you're going to want this to be something that you could invite contractors or employees to use as you grow and that is also very easy to access wherever you are. The system you choose has to have the ability to work from your laptop or desktop as well as your smartphone.

I currently use Harvest because it is simple, easily shared, and has the ability to not only generate reports on the amount of a project budget that has been spent, but it will even send me an e-mail as I start to come to the end of the allotted resources.

Once you have your timekeeping system in place, use it religiously, even to track nonclient time—like the time you spend on sales, operations, or the many other activities it takes to keep the enterprise going. These are all costs that need to be understood and figure into your profitability. This is going to take some effort to habituate—time tracking is not common in the nonprofit and education worlds, so you may want to start with a recurring appointment or a to-do item reminding you multiple times a day to ensure you are updating your time. Resist the temptation to figure out everything at the end of the day—despite the best intentions, I've found people rarely perceive the time they spend on tasks well and easily forget how they spent parts of their day.

ELEMENT FOUR: A CLOUD-COMPUTING SYSTEM

Cloud computing can help you easily keep your files off-site and safe. Cloud computing is inexpensive, simple, and vital if you have a team that you're working with or if you want to easily collaborate with clients without having to constantly send files back and forth.

Many consultants don't think about file storage or sharing. They take the easiest route possible and use their hard drive to store everything. But that's a dangerous approach, because if your laptop is lost or computer is ruined, you lose everything. I strongly recommend using one of the many secure, cloud-based file services that are out there. The current major options are Google Drive, Dropbox, iCloud, or OneDrive. I happen to use Dropbox but have used the others and find them all comparable. The key is having one place where your files are stored off-site. The result is that they are safer, easier to access, and simpler to share. The last two points are particularly significant. Many times, I have been on the road and for one reason or another had to use a client or hotel computer. Using Dropbox, I can easily access any file and know it will be saved for access when I return home.

Cloud-based file systems also allow easy sharing to clients and colleagues. It is easy to grant anyone—contractors, employees, or even clients—specific access to some or all files. Since the results are all saved to the cloud, you instantly have the latest edits whenever you need them.

ELEMENT FIVE: TELEPHONE, E-MAIL, AND CALENDAR—GETTING THAT BIG COMPANY FEEL

Chances are, whatever your specialization is within the nonprofit world, you are going to be spending a lot of time talking and meeting with people. This reality affects you as a consultant in two ways. First, there's the issue of time—it seems like a simple issue, but the time it takes to manage all these things can be consuming. Second, telephone, e-mail, and calendar appointments and scheduling are a key part of your clients' experience. There's an opportunity here to really differentiate yourself by using technology so that clients have the same experience with you that they would with any large consultancy, without you or them having to pay for it.

For e-mail, there are a lot of options out there for hosting. I have used Gmail since the beginning because of Gmail's reliability, ease of use (not only for you but when you add others), and cost (Google offers inexpensive, expandable business packages). You can easily find a mail host. More important is that you choose an option that allows you to set up and use a "domained e-mail," one with your own company name (e.g., @civstrat.com). Most consultants don't take this route but instead use the "public" domain (e.g., @gmail.com or @hotmail.com). It is not difficult to set up or costly to pay for a domain (Gmail's small-business packages can help you do it), and the benefit for branding and professional presentation will differentiate you from competitors.

When you do set up your domain, make it relevant to your company by linking to either the firm's name (in our case "civstrat.com" for Civitas Strategies) or the type of work you do (so our company might use "nonprofitstrategyexperts.com"). Also, think about the suffix. There's a proliferation of different ones, but the reality is ".com" is still by far the most prevalent and easy to use. Using others can lead to errors. One firm I worked with a few years ago had a ".co" and invariably would lose e-mail because people assumed it was a typo and added the "m" for ".com."

When you set up your telephones, again, there are a lot of choices for providers—landline, cable, and mobile. Get a service that augments your phones and leverages your time. For the individual consultant, consider Google Voice or a similar service. Google Voice is free and provides two great services. First, it gives your clients one number to call that will forward them as you direct (to your cell, landline, or both at once). The result for your client is ease of contact. I tell my clients, "Call that one number, and you will get me anywhere in the world." That's a powerful statement on service! Also, Google Voice offers automatic transcription of voice mail, and it does a pretty good job. Accordingly, if I am in a situation where I can't check voice mail, at least I can quickly read the message and know if it requires an urgent response.

Grasshopper provides consultants with a sense of being a larger, unified company by providing a central phone number where callers can then be connected to team members wherever they are. I don't use it, but if I did, clients could call one number and get a phone tree to select who they wanted to talk to. When selected, they would be forwarded to the phone, cell or landline, used by that person. The result is an easy connection for clients and a "big office" feel.

The last, but certainly not least, component of creating your robot office is your system for setting and tracking appointments. As a consultant, you are selling your time, and every minute that passes unused is gone forever. So time is very precious to you. Concurrently, there are going to be many draws on your time. Generally, consultants meet and talk a lot—in person, by phone, and by videoconference. In the public-service world, where communication and process are highly valued, there tends to be even more engagement. Accordingly, even managing your time can be, well...time consuming.

As for where you put your appointments, there are a lot of options out there: Outlook, Google Calendar, iCal, Sunrise, and others. (As others are developed, I will include them on our website.) The most important aspect of your calendar is that it is easy for you to understand, manage, and share with others.

The bigger issue is how you schedule your time. Scheduling seems simple, but it is one of the largest infrastructure time sucks for consultants. And remember—every minute you spend scheduling, you are not creating obvious value for your clients. Even when it seems small, it adds up. For example, as part of our approach, we conduct about three hundred qualitative interviews per year. We spend about fifteen minutes scheduling each, on average. That is forty-five hundred minutes a year—almost ten full working days of time annually, and this is just qualitative interviews (it doesn't include scheduling group meetings, one-on-one meetings and planning sessions, coaching, etc.).

The time adds up quickly, so I recommend getting a system like Doodle that allows you to easily set meetings. When you e-mail a Doodle poll, meeting participants receive a number of time options, and they then indicate when they are available. The result is a quick, visual summary of which times work best for everyone attending.

Another emerging technology to consider is Amy.x.ai. Amy is a cloud artificial-intelligence assistant. To use Amy, you copy her on an e-mail, and then Amy works with meeting participants via e-mail to set an appointment. Whatever you choose, make sure it's clean and understandable. Also know that it's not going to be fool-proof—some people will balk at using a Doodle poll or just plain won't understand the system, in which case you may need to just call and open your calendars. Despite this, upward of 80 percent of the time, technology will be used as intended and save you a great deal of time.

Keep in mind, some of the five elements of the robot office can be addressed by the same online system or software, and others may require multiple solutions. By completing exercise eight, you can quickly make these selections step by step.

EXERCISE EIGHT: CREATING YOUR ROBOT OFFICE

Each step in creating the robot office will take well under an hour, but the decision process may take longer. Though there is an investment of time in deciding and acting on each step, the time and money you will save later is well worth it.

- **Step One: Find Your Space**—One of the greatest small-business costs (and therefore an impact on profitability and sustainability) is office space. Whenever possible, I encourage clients to find the least expensive solution possible. Start by asking yourself, "Do I really need office space?" The single greatest reason to have office space is to meet and work with clients. Your answer will probably fit into one of four categories:
  - ○ **I plan to meet clients at my own office on a regular basis**—Then by all means find a commercial space. This could be a traditional office, or you may want to consider a coworking space, where you can lease an office and share common spaces, such as conference rooms.
  - ○ **I plan to meet clients at my own office occasionally**—You can get a traditional office, but coworking space or subletting an office from another business will probably be more cost effective.
  - ○ **I don't plan to meet with clients on-site**—Consider working from your home. You are already paying for the space, so there's no additional cost. And, if you qualify for a home-office deduction, it can actually save you money. If you go this route, try to set a space for your use—even if it is just a desk in a common room. Having one spot where you can keep everything handy will make your life a lot easier.
  - ○ **I don't plan to meet with clients on-site, but I don't have the space at home**—I'd try to push for the free options mentioned previously. There is probably a coffee shop, library, or other area where you can work uninterrupted free of charge.
- **Step Two: Count All the Beans (Money and Hours)**—Profitability is crucial for your business, so you need to be able to track your hours, costs, revenues, and expenses as well as easily and quickly invoice (to keep money flowing in). There are two ways to do all of this, and both are based on one question: Do you have an accountant or bookkeeper? I'll talk more in section three about

when to get specialized help, such as an accountant or a bookkeeper, but for now, let's answer the question based on your current configuration.

- **I am doing it all myself**—Consider a simple-to-use, all-in-one system, like FreshBooks. The advantage of a system like FreshBooks is that it is intended to be used by solo entrepreneurs and very small businesses, including consultancies; will have everything you need; automatically downloads from your accounts; tracks your revenues and expenses; keeps hours and monitors project budgets; and has one of the easiest invoicing interfaces I've seen. For the first four years, I used FreshBooks exclusively and can't say enough good things about it. The only reason I switched is that I stopped doing the books myself.

- **I have a bookkeeper and an accountant helping me**—Chances are they're going to want you to use QuickBooks. As I mentioned before, I'm not a huge fan of QuickBooks and changed over begrudgingly when I took on an accountant and bookkeeper. It is the industry standard, and that has some advantages, including the easy ability of your accountant/bookkeeper to get in and help you manage the books as needed. However, the interface is not as simple as FreshBooks, and there's no negative timekeeping system. Accordingly, if you choose QuickBooks, you should look at an outside system to track your time. I currently use Harvest, which is very helpful and easy to use.

- **Step three: Clouds and the "Big Company" Feel**—I suggest addressing robot-office elements four and five in three steps.

  - **Decide on your e-mail system**—You are going to send a lot of e-mails, and so you want to be very comfortable with that system. Chances are this will also drive your choice of calendar, since they are often integrated. Make sure you add branding to your system—your logo if possible, and a signature line with your contact information. Do the same to the calendar system as well so your clients have a consistent experience.

  - **Select the cloud-computing system**—Play around with the major options online first to see which one is most comfortable for you. Remember, as you grow, there may be other team members using it, and you may want to share files with your client, so make sure that the system is as simple to use as possible.

○ **Select a telephone provider and appointment-setting service**—Now you're ready to select a telephone provider and use an additional service like Google Voice or Grasshopper. With your calendar up and running, you can also consider adding Doodle or Amy.x.ai to help you manage the calendar system you have set up.

Section II: Get Customers

W hew—you made it! Your company has been created, and you have a robot office ready to support you. Now the doors are open, and you need to get your first customers.

In this section, I will help you not only bring in your initial clients but also create a pipeline of sales that will sustain and expand your business. I am going to start with the basic tools you need for your sales and marketing, including a logo and a website. I will cover how to come up with your prices and structure projects and introduce the Bull's-eye, a simple, time-tested strategy for driving your sales and marketing. Finally, I will review the Pemberton Method for tracking and valuing your pipeline of prospects.

ANOTHER DIRTY WORD: SALES

I have found that, in particular, consultants to nonprofits are loathe to use the word "sales." Instead there is a tendency to use "marketing" to mean both sales and marketing. In truth, they are two different sets of activities related to the same thing—helping people and organizations solve problems. Understanding that last part is crucial— sales and marketing are not about hoodwinking someone out of money or going door to door selling your services at random. If they are done correctly, sales and marketing are about finding people who need your help and helping them.

I need you to get over the sales stigma—it is a core vehicle for scaling your social impact. If you want to help children, save the environment, or realize any of your dreams, you need to sell your services or products to nonprofits. A friend who was a top salesperson for a Fortune 500 company told me that she loved selling because she loved solving people's problems by selling the right solutions for those problems. You need to realize that, as a consultant, you are in sales, and that's all right.

With that out of the way, let's focus on defining both concepts. Marketing is a set of efforts that creates the condition for the sale. Sales are the activities with a specific person or organization that lead to an exchange of goods and services. Let's take an example that is near and dear to my heart every winter in the Northeast—snowblowers. A television commercial for snowblowers is marketing. It reminds me that winter is coming and prompts my recall that I need a replacement. When I head down to my local hardware store, the sales process begins. The salesperson learns about what I need, like a little power on a steep driveway, and suggests models. When I find the right one, the sales process concludes with the store owner gaining a sale, and I get to go home and rest easy knowing I am ready for the next onslaught of snow.

Throughout, you'll see me reference "sales and marketing" over the traditional "marketing and sales." Yes, marketing comes before sales in the process, but I do this to remind you that it is all about sales. Marketing is great only if it gets you the sale; otherwise, it is a waste of your time. Accordingly, I always want you to think about sales as the more crucial goal of the two.

For the consultant, the principles of sales and marketing are the same, but the scale and resources are much lower. I'll talk more about a methodology for targeting prospective clients later in this section, but for now, know that most of you are going to target ten or twenty clients a year, rather than selling one hundred thousand snow-blowers. In terms of resources, to keep your profit high, you'll need to have a lean sales and marketing budget. I'll talk later, not about television ads like in the snow-blower example but about the use of relationships and low-/no-cost strategies to connect with those who need your services most. The lack of resources and cash flow, as I described earlier, should have you tracking your time to conversion (i.e., the time it takes from when you first have contact with a prospective customer until you make the sale). Sales can, but usually don't, happen overnight. In our work with consultancies, I've found that more typically it takes four to nine months from initial contact to sale. This is a consideration not only for how you use resources and manage cash but also for how you manage your overall sales pipeline, since you will always need to think months in advance.

WHO ARE YOU SELLING TO ANYWAY?

Another set of often misused terms are "customer" (or "client") and "consumer," which is ironic since the difference is particularly relevant to the social-impact world. Your customer is the person who purchases your goods and services. The consumer is the one who uses them. Many times, your customer and consumer are the same.

Let me give you a simple example. I like pizza. Let's say I go into a pizza shop and buy three slices—one for me and one for each of my sons. When I buy the slices, I am the customer—I hand over the money and receive my lunch in return. However, when we eat them, all three of us are consumers (even though I was the only customer).

This may seem like semantics, but in the nonprofit world, this difference comes into play much more often, since in many cases your customers and consumers are different. For example, a philanthropic foundation (the customer) may hire you to manage a collective-impact process among a group of community organizations (the consumers). The result is that in some cases you have to make two "sales"—the customer, who has the means for your engagement, but also the consumers, who may influence the customer's choices. However, just convincing the consumer of your value alone won't make your sale—you always need the customer to decide in your favor.

Here are some other examples of my clients' customers and consumers to bring home the concept:

Customers	Consumers
Executive Director	Staff
School District Director of Professional Development	Principals and Teachers
College Center Director	Mid-level management
Parents of young children	Parents of young children (they are both customer and consumer for this product)
State Education Agencies	School Districts statewide

Note that the customer isn't always in the top position in the organizational structure (e.g., the school-district director of professional development). This illustrates one of the complexities of selling—the customer may not always be clear. You may know that Organization A, for example, wants your services, but who at Organization

A has the authority to decide on a purchase? This is a key point since it can delay or even derail your sales process. Sometimes people will spend months wooing a person only to find out their prospect now has to take it to his or her boss. You then enter a whole new process, delaying the time to sale and increasing the risk that the sale will never happen.

4

The Toolbox

There are a many trappings of a large company that I eschew, but there is a basic "toolbox" that contains marketing, branding, and sales tools that are crucial investments. Specifically, I recommend a toolbox consisting of the following:

- logo
- business cards
- company bio
- website

Similar to the MVC, I have found these tools are the minimum you need to have prior to pursuing clients, and these tools may even give you an edge. They help your customers know you are a "real" business (which also differentiates you from many of the consultancies in the nonprofit world that lack some or all of these tools), and, most importantly, they give you the confidence to sell by knowing what to say and having a professional appearance.

BASIC BRANDING

The first step is designing your logo—this can range from simple to complex. The objective isn't to have the end-all of logos; you don't want to hold up your whole business for it. Instead, have an image that you like and that projects professionalism. That may seem obvious, but I have seen many entrepreneurs become logo obsessed—missing the forest for the trees. That being the case, refresh your logo every three to five years to ensure it stays current and distinctive.

There are a lot of resources for logo design. There are even options to engage a professional designer that are not that expensive, so don't panic. There are basically three options—self-designing, using a graphic artist, and crowd designing.

You can self-design a simple logo using a site like GraphicSprings. When I first started out with Romano Consulting, I used a similar site to design my first logo. On the positive side, it was clean and simple, and I received a number of compliments on it. I even remember on one flight talking to a nonprofit leader in the same row, and he couldn't believe that I had done it myself. From start to finish, it took about twenty minutes and $200. However, it wasn't unique, nor did it speak specifically to my firm and vision.

When I changed to Civitas Strategies, I opted for the second route, engaging a professional graphic artist. It was more expensive than self-design, for us about two and a half times—and the price range for designers can get fairly high. I also liked being able to talk to the artist about specific ideas I wanted to convey. Remember that when seeking a designer, the taste and skills of graphic artists can vary, so start by asking for recommendations from your network, and review samples of their work extensively.

I used the third option, crowd design, in 2014 when I did a logo refresh. This time I used 99Designs. My experiences then, and subsequently with 99Designs, have been so positive that I would suggest it now as a starting point for a logo design. The prices are reasonable, and you only pay when you have a logo you like.

Through 99Designs, hundreds of graphic artists around the world develop logos (and redevelop them repeatedly based on your feedback), so you get many choices with very different styles. It also offers a simple way to engage peers, clients, and others in your network to vote on different options. This not only gives you rapid, external feedback but also builds support for your venture as people become interested in the project.

In using 99Designs for my own firm or clients' organizations, I have found it is most successful when you provide examples of the logos you like up front and a lot of feedback along the way. Be prepared to log in two or three times a day to provide feedback. The projects are usually a quick turnaround (less than a week), and the feedback makes a tremendous difference. I also have had great experiences using the poll function to garner the input of clients and colleagues. During the 2014 logo refresh, this feedback was instrumental since I was able to hear not only my clients' feedback on the logo but their perceptions of our company's value. For example, one reviewer pointed out the logo we ended up selecting and currently use show how we lift up our clients. That's not only important feedback but an insight into clients' perceptions.

With your logo you can easily get business cards. Yes, I know—in this day and age, it seems anachronistic. The reality is that they are still used and have a certain weight in defining a "legitimate" business. There's also a simple practicality to it—when you are out and about, for example, at a conference and somebody wants your contact information, having a card at the ready can be easier and faster than finding a paper or pen or even using an instant transfer like iOS's AirDrop. Not everyone has mobile technology, but everyone can accept a business card.

I suggest keeping it simple—no need to add a photo or print on the highest-grade paper. Just include the basics—logo, name, address, phone number, e-mail, social-media handles, and website. You can get business cards printed at almost any printer locally or online. I have had a lot of success over the years using Vistaprint, which has simple tools to put together your own cards, has a good product at a good price, and delivers quickly.

GETTING THE WORD OUT

Your next tool, the company bio, is essentially a document containing the type of information you find on most websites: who you are, what you do, and who you've done it for. Yes, these are on your web page, but half the time that people want this information, they want it in a document. This is particularly true of nonprofit leaders, who tend to prefer documents over web pages.

There is also a value to attaching it to every proposal you produce. You may know potential customers well, but you never know whom they are going to share proposals with (e.g., board members, staff, or volunteers) for opinions. These others may have no idea who you are, so having your bio attached can help distinguish you from competitors.

I had a colleague not too long ago who didn't include her company bio with a proposal. She was very confident that the recipient of the proposal didn't need to know more information since they had known each other for more than ten years. However, my colleague did not realize that her prospective client was going to have to share the proposal with her board. Once the board had seen it, two weeks later at their next meeting, they had a lot of questions as to why they should engage this company. Unfortunately, my colleague's prospective client could not articulate that well. As a result, the proposal was rejected, and a new one had to be developed in response to the board's questions. My colleague was eventually selected for the project, but this process added almost three months of time to a sale, which may have been mitigated by attaching the company bio.

EXERCISE NINE: BUILDING YOUR COMPANY BIO

Develop your bio in three steps. Each step will take about an hour. Don't try to complete this in one day—you'll want some time in between, even twenty-four to forty-eight hours, to ensure you have fresh eyes and a clear head.

- **Step One: Pull the Essentials**—Answer the following five questions in an electronic document or on a piece of paper. Be as succinct as possible, and use the information you collected in section one, especially your charter:
  - What does your company do—overall, but also your key services and products?
  - What value do you generate?
  - How are you different from other firms?
  - Who has used your products and services?
  - Who are the principals of the firm (i.e., the biographies of your key personnel)?
- **Step Two: Write it Out**—Transform the questions into a concise document. As a starting point, these questions could be turned into section headers. Keep three other points in mind while you build it.

  First, be concise—this should not be more than two pages, and if it is one or one and a half, all the better. The longer the document is, the more you will lose people along the way. I know that many of you will counter with how crucial the details of your work are. You must know this is not *your* document but one meant to communicate with often busy, distracted leaders. If you want them to really hear you, the document will need to be tight.

  Second, to the previous point, this is a key external-communication piece, so share it with critical friends—at least four or five—prior to sharing it with a potential client. Invariably, your critical friends will find ways to greatly improve the document's effectiveness.

  Third, when you discuss previous projects, consider a simple, three-sentence format where the first tells the reader the condition of your client's problem ahead of your arrival, then tell what you did, and finally end with the result (preferably with some measure of success). For example, "Organization X was struggling with how it could increase the impact of its services without additional funds. We helped the organization see an implementable, cost-effective approach to scaling that still had a significant impact on the families it served. In the past five years, Organization X has been able to double its service levels and expand to two new states using the near approach."

- **Step Three: Get Perspective**—Have someone else, a critical friend, especially one who has used your services, review the document. Ask three questions:
  - ○ Did the document clearly convey the value they believe that you have?
  - ○ Was it compelling enough to warrant investing in your services?
  - ○ Does your firm seem different from others out there?

When you are finished, make sure you use your logo on it and brand it in other ways (such as the use of color in section headings) so that it is clearly from your firm.

A WEBSITE: BASIC CREDIBILITY

Thirty years ago, if you didn't have an office, potential customers would probably question the viability and seriousness of your firm. As I discussed earlier, that has changed significantly. Of similar import now is a website. Ironically, despite the importance of having a web page, only about 30 percent (my rough estimation, based on my experience) of consultancies serving nonprofits have one. This is a reflection of the perceived complexity and cost of web design and hosting. In reality, just like the many innovations that support the robot office, it has never been easier or less expensive to launch a high-quality site.

When you look at most websites now, they are either e-commerce sites (like Amazon, where you buy things), information platforms (such as YouTube, where users can upload and stream videos or other media), or a business description (like ours at Civitas Strategies). The former two can have some technical complexities and costs (though even e-commerce sites are getting easier and less expensive to build), but really what you need is the last one—a spot in cyberspace that gives users some information about who you are and what you do and assures them that you are a "legitimate" business.

Start first with the text—basically you want to reproduce your company bio on the web. You'll want to expand on it—for example, adding some client stories, testimonials, or pictures (see our Civitas Strategies website at http://civstrat.com/, which is an expansion of our company bio) and at the same time cut it down (e.g., converting a lot of the dense text to bullets). Also, ensure that there is an easy way for people to reach out for more information (such as a Contact Us page). Finally, you'll want to add photographs and other images as appropriate.

Similar to the logo, you can build your own website or engage a professional designer. Start with a serious look at the existing self-design options, such as Wix, Weebly, or GoDaddy. Unfortunately, when I think of self-design, my mind goes to the primitive resources available in the late 1990s when I created my first sites and I was programming code in HTML. However, like the rest of the technology available to you, website technology is light years from those initial tools. Now you have the ability to easily customize modern, clean templates quickly. When I developed the *Small But Mighty* website (www.smallbutmightybook.com), I was so impressed with the templates available that I almost created the site using one instead of a designer.

We did take a different course with the Civitas Strategies website. When we first developed it in 2010, we opted to use a local design firm. I liked that we were able to have the ability to customize the site in every way. Overall, the experience was fine, but I didn't think it was worth the investment of time and money. We were directing a lot of the process. In the end we got a page that was fine, but it was far from a showpiece. In our 2015 website relaunch, we again used 99Designs. The experience was similar to the logo refresh—we received a lot of great options and were able to refine them to a look we really liked. There was still a significant effort by our team in driving the process, but the results were much more impressive and unique.

5

Pricing

Your toolbox is ready to market and sell your services, but there's one more step to take before signing that first customer—being clear on how you are going to charge your fees, including how you structure projects.

HOW MUCH?

One of the questions that I get from novice and seasoned consultants alike is, "How much should I charge?" It is a crucial question—the long-term viability of your business and livelihood depend on it. Most consultants in the nonprofit market are daunted by the challenge of determining a market rate, so they guess, and typically that guess is too low. I have helped clients review their rates over the past seven years. The consultants I served were, on average, underpricing 33 percent below market rate, some underpricing as low as 45 percent below market. When they did raise their rates (incrementally, over a few months), their sales didn't suffer. Nothing changed except that they were able to realize stronger revenue.

In determining your rate, there are really two separate questions to answer:

1. What is the rate I should use to estimate my costs for a project?
2. What should I charge a client based on that rate?

The two questions are both necessary and very different. They really reflect the two sides of profit—your costs and your revenue. Let's take a closer look at each and how to determine the "goldilocks rate" for your firm—one that is not so high you lose work but high enough to cover your costs and generate the profit you need for the long term.

COSTING YOUR COSTS

Let's calculate how much your services should cost. You'll want to pull together your financial information ahead of time—budget and actual costs for this year and last year. If you are just starting out, you'll need to estimate your budget (more on that later). This will take some time, so allow yourself an hour or two and have someone check your calculations. Even if you are a math whiz, mistakes can happen, and the answers to the steps that follow will form the financial foundation of your business model's potential success or failure.

Start by thinking about your basic operational needs—ensuring you cover the costs to keep your doors open. This may not be obvious—many times consultants don't keep all the costs in mind or the amount of time they can't bill (because they are selling or recruiting an associate or fixing the printer and such). The result can easily be the Hamster archetype, where it seems like you have to work so much to just break even.

There are a number of ways to calculate an hourly cost. I'm going to run through what I think is the simplest to calculate and that will be useful for your business: take your overhead and divide by the total billable hours, and then add hourly personnel cost to that total: (total overhead cost ÷ total billable hours) + hourly personnel cost = total hourly cost.

Step One: Calculate Your Total Overhead

Your overhead costs are ones that apply to the overall operation of your company, not just one project. Many of these are part of the MVC—such as paying your web server, accountant, or corporate-filing fees. But not all of your overhead costs are in your MVC. Two key ones to consider are your personal-development expenses (like sending an employee or yourself to training) and any sales and marketing costs. For personal development, include any costs for training, conferences, and association memberships that are crucial for your business. Health-care expenses, or other similar benefits that are at one price for the whole company, should also be included here. Make sure you ask yourself the "crucial question," because we always want to keep profitability in mind, so the overhead costs in this area are not about what would be fun, but rather what helps you to sell more work or do your work more effectively. For sales and marketing, include any travel necessary to meet with potential clients and the cost of materials like brochures, if you have them.

To recap, overhead costs should include all of those nonproject costs, such as the following:

○ office space (e.g., if you go that route or even the rent you may pay yourself for your home office)
○ utilities (e.g., electric, gas, telephones, Internet)
○ equipment (e.g., computers, printers)
○ consumables (e.g., paper, printer ink)
○ professional fees and development
○ business taxes

For our example, let's assume the overhead totals $55,000.

Step Two: Calculate Your Billable Hours

You want to take the overhead cost and make an hourly overhead cost out of it, so you need to determine how many hours in total everyone on your team will be actually consulting and billing. Start off with the total hours each person on the team will be contributing to the firm. You may have historical data on how you are using your hours that you can draw from. If you do, great! If not, assume, after vacation and sick leave, only about 70 percent of your and any principal's hours, 80 percent of employees' hours, and 85–90 percent of contractors' hours are billable.

For our example, let's assume that your firm comprises you, an employee, and a contractor. You and the employee work forty hours a week and get three weeks' vacation and one-week sick leave every year.

52 weeks/year × 40 work hours/week = 2,080 hours
3 weeks/year × 40 vacation hours/week = 120 hours
1 week sick days/year x 40 hours/week = 40 hours

2,080 hours − 120 hours − 40 hours = **1,920 potentially billable hours per principal and employee**

Of that, only 70 percent of your hours and 80 percent of your employees' hours will be billable.

> 1,920 potentially billable hours × 0.70 = **1,344 billable hours/principal**
> 1,920 potentially billable hours × 0.80 = **1,536 billable hours/employee**

For consultants, let's say you are going to occasionally engage them for an average of ten hours a week, which means they will be used 520 hours a year, 90 percent of which will be billable.

> 10 hours/week = 520 hours/year x 0.9 = **468 billable hours/contractor**

When you add the billable hours for each of you together, you get the hours that will be billed overall.

> 1,344 + 1,536 + 468 = **3,348 billable hours for your company**

This is another calculation where you need to be very honest with yourself about your lifestyle-design goals to come up with a useful estimate. If you plan to only work three days a week, eight hours a day, with four weeks' vacation, that means you only have 1,152 hours to work with. Yes, there are weeks you may work more, but there are also weeks you may work less because you are sick or the boiler in your house breaks—life happens. (You are also going to have a greater role in sales, marketing, and running the business.) In this case, that means 345.6 of your 1,152 hours will be part of your overhead.

Step Three: Calculate Your Hourly Overhead

- When you have the billable hours (i.e., the hours for each person per year, less the ones that are not billable) for each person, total them all—this is the total number of billable hours—and divide the overhead by this number. In other words, take your overhead cost, and divide it by the total billable hours to get an hourly rate. Let's use the $55,000 overhead cost from the example in step one and the 3,348 in billable hours from step two. You now have an approximate overhead cost per every hour anyone is billing.

$55,000 ÷ 3,348 = **$16.43 hourly overhead cost**

Step Four: Calculate Your Personnel Cost

Now let's calculate an hourly personnel cost for each person. The method will vary by the type of resource:

- For the principals/owners of the firm (potentially just you but also any other partners), add together your salary, payroll and other taxes, benefits (e.g., contributions to retirement), and the minimum net profit you will need to continue the venture. This last point can be difficult—especially in the non-profit world, we tend to feel like we are being greedy to talk about profit. This is far from the case—you need to make a living. You need to clearly ask yourself how much compensation makes this venture worth the time, effort, and risk. Maybe it isn't much more than your salary; maybe the inse-curity of life as an entrepreneur makes you want more. Only you know the answer.

  As an example, let's say you really want $80,000 in salary, have to pay $15,000 for benefits, and want a minimum of $10,000 in net profits. That means a base of $105,000. Regardless of the answer, be honest with your-self. I've seen many a venture serving nonprofits where the principals weren't honest up front and then later found themselves disappointed in their compensation.
  - For salaried employees, include their total compensation for the year—sal-ary, any benefits, payroll taxes, and possible bonus or deferred compensa-tion.
  - For contractors, use their hourly rate multiplied by the total hours you plan to use them for the year.

For each role, divide their cost by the total billable hours you plan for them in the upcoming year.

Next add the overhead hourly rate to the hourly cost for each person—now you have an hourly cost. Any revenue per hour less than this number means you are likely losing money.

For our example, let's still assume you have one principal, one employee, and one contractor. Keep in mind the billable hours from step two: 1,344/principal, 1,536/employee, and 468/contractor.

> One principal = $80,000 salary + $15,000 benefits + $10,000 net profit = **$105,000 base**
>
> $105,000 base ÷ 1,344 billable hours = **$78.13/hour**
>
> One employee = $65,000 salary + $13,000 benefits + $5,000 taxes + $5,000 bonus = **$88,000 base**
>
> $88,000 base ÷ 1,536 billable hours = **$57.29/hour**
>
> One contractor = $40/hour × 10 hours/week × 52 weeks = **$20,800 base**
>
> $20,800 ÷ 468 = **$44.44/hour**

Step Five: Create Your Total Hourly Cost

For each resource, add the hourly overhead and the hourly personnel cost. Now you have it—an hourly cost for each person!

To finish with our example, this means (refer to steps three and four) the following:

o For you: $16.43 + $78.13 = **$94.56**
o For the employee: $16.43 + $57.29 = **$73.72**
o For the contractor: $16.43 + $44.44 = **$60.87**

Whew! You made it through the first half—now on to your fee!

FROM COST TO FEE

After all that work on your cost, we are now ready to think about what you should be charging. But here's the kicker—this is really more art than science.

There are so many variables that come into play in determining your fee, from the demand and criticality of your services to the prices of other competitors and options to the available funding. Also, you may want to have some form of reserve included to address the unexpected and a net profit (remember, we only built a baseline compensation for you into costs—you may and should want more than the minimum).

The next question then is, if there are so many variables, how do I price?

Start by understanding the current pricing in the market. This can be as simple as asking potential customers what they are paying or even other consultants. This information will give you a sense of what the market is currently paying; however, you'll want a few data points and also want to be sure they are analogous to you and your firm (see more in exercise ten).

Then, choose a method for pricing. There are many methodologies. I'm going to focus on the most common and most useful ones:

- **Full budget** is when you develop a budget for your whole organization, including a profit target to reward you and your staff, a contingency for any problems for the organization, and everything else that profit could be used to mitigate or build. As a "numbers person," I used to espouse this approach, and it is what I used for the first two years of Civitas Strategies. But I've found over the years that there is so much you cannot plan for, and as a result, your budget at the start of the year doesn't resemble year-end.
- **The multiplier** is setting your fee at 1.5, 2, 2.5, or 3 times your costs per hour. In the previous example, our principal's cost per hour was $94.56. Using this method, the fee per hour would be $142, $189, $236, and $284, respectively. This may seem way too simplistic, but I have found over the years a 1.5, 2, or 2.5 multiplier to be the most effective method—it is easy to implement and tends to cover your existing costs and surprises along the way, and it results in a profit to build the business and reward your and your staff's efforts.

- **The burdened principal** is rarely used now. In this method, the principals (you and the other most senior consultants) would have a rate that includes part of the cost of everyone else who supports your work. In other words, clients pay for your hourly rate and get all the support figured into it (including any mid- or entry-level consultants, administrative support, contractors, etc., that will be needed to do the work). Using the numbers we calculated in step five, that means you would charge $229.15 ($94.56 + 73.72 + 60.87) per hour. Avoid this method at all costs—you are burying a lot of costs and charging a very high fee in a very price-sensitive sector.

Finally, check the fee, based on whichever method you used, against the market range from your research. You'll want to try to be in the average fee uncovered in your research. Keep to that rule—if you are lower, raise it to the average! You can always change your fee and lower it if you have to, but as mentioned previously, most consultants in the nonprofit sector are underpricing, not overpricing.

EXERCISE TEN: SETTING YOUR FEE

Let's calculate how much you should charge. I'm going to use the multiplier method since it is the easiest and usually hits a reasonable rate. Now that you have your hourly cost (step five in the previous section), this will go pretty quickly. Step one will be the longest—probably two to three hours of conversations and e-mails—but the rest can be done in thirty minutes or so.

- **Step One: Research Rates**—When you had your initial conversations about your value, you may have also collected some information on your competitors' pricing. If you did, include it in the mix. Regardless, find pricing for at least five analogous firms (ones that are around the same size and offering similar services). Also, listen carefully to the skill level associated with the rate. Are they talking about an entry-level or senior-level person? Make sure you know so you can align them with your team and their rates.

  To get the information, reach out to friends and colleagues who hire or whose organizations hire similar consultants. You can tell them you just need a range, not names of firms. Another way is to ask what they think is a reasonable hourly rate for your service. You also can ask other consultants in your network—the worst-case scenario is that they say no, but most are open about it since they tell clients all the time (so it is public). For example, at Civitas Strategies, we are totally transparent about our billing. If another consultant asks, I am happy to share our current rates—just e-mail me at gary@smallbutmightybook.com (there—you'll have one set of numbers already). Take all your numbers, and note the average rate among your data points.
- **Step Two: Multiply**—Multiply your hourly costs by 1.5, 2, 2.5, and 3, and round up to the nearest $25 (e.g., if you had $189, as we did, your rate would be $200). Compare the rate to the midpoint of the rates in step one. Again, move up or down from the midpoint as you need to.

  If you can't get enough data, or any at all, bypass step one, and just do step two. It's better if you have some market information, but if you don't and your fees are over market, your prospective clients will let you know!

  This is not a one-time exercise. Your costs and the market will shift, so do this at least once a year.

6

Structuring and Estimating Projects

You have a fee that is based on your real costs—you're almost ready to start pricing out proposals for your prospective clients. The next step is to talk about the different types of pricing structures and then determine how to pull these into an estimate.

There are really three ways to structure the fees for your projects. You can use one of the following:

1. Hourly agreement
2. Pay one price
3. Value pricing

Let's look at each in more detail.

HOURLY AGREEMENT

An hourly agreement is as straightforward as it sounds—you're going to charge your client by using your hourly rate as you accrue the time on work performed. Very often you will have an upper limit where you need to alert your client or stop work, but the agreement will almost always end your commitment at that level (i.e., when the hours are spent or you hit the cost ceiling, you stop working). The key advantage of this structure is that it mitigates much of your risk—if the client decides to use you more than intended or shift the nature of the project, you are covered.

Probably the most difficult part is when you start running close to your ceiling or accruing more hours than anticipated. The disadvantage is that you can become a bit like a faucet, where your client turns your hours on and off when needed, rather than based on a plan or an agreed to project. Yes, your risks on cost overruns are mitigated, but it is difficult to have staff respond to on-demand needs and also provide services to all your existing clients.

Despite the risks of varied usage, an hourly agreement tends to be the most advantageous to consultants.

PAY ONE PRICE

The second way to structure your contracts is the most common: pay one price. With this structure, you agree to a scope of work and a set fee (which may or may not include your expenses). The advantage of this structure is that you know up front what you will be doing and when you will do it, so there are fewer unexpected twists and turns that could impact other projects (such as with an hourly contract, where you may have no work one day and too much the next). There's also an opportunity to increase profitability—if you can complete the scope of work faster or more efficiently, you can realize a larger profit.

However, you are also assuming a great deal of risk. The project may be more complicated than you thought and now you either have to convince your client that the scope has changed and is worth more money or have to live with it, which means the project is less profitable. Also, there is the risk of a client engaging in scope creep: the incremental expansion of the project work without changing the price. Scope creep can be insidious, especially if you are very focused on trying to create value for clients whenever possible.

Here's an example that comes up in my work for Civitas Strategies all the time—increased interviews. As mentioned previously, we gather qualitative data for our clients using one-on-one interviews. Our clients greatly value this service since our team is highly skilled at collecting information from interviewees, especially data they may not normally reveal to our clients. When I create a pay-one-price proposal, I include how many interviews we will do in the scope. However, once we have the project and begin to add interviewees, our clients get excited, often wanting to add one or two more. And there is the scope creep—we went from the fifteen interviews, which were in the cost estimate, to seventeen.

Scope creep can be small for a given activity, but if it happens often enough, it adds up and could have an impact on your bottom line.

I've met many consultants over the years, especially in the nonprofit world, who see scope creep happening and know they need to do something but are hesitant about talking to clients about changes and avoid it at all costs. My suggestion: get over it! I've talked to clients about scope creep many times over the years, and I have never had clients run away, cancel a contract, or even raise their voice. Actually, it has been the exact opposite—most of the time clients didn't realize what was happening and wanted to readjust the scope, either by retracting the request or by expanding the contract. In fact, it is more commonly the latter—leading to more revenue, not less. I repeat: more revenue, not less!

VALUE PRICING

The third structure is value pricing—this is one that you hear a lot about, especially in the past few years, but frankly I think it is pretty difficult to pull off ethically in the nonprofit world. Value-pricing advocates suggest throwing away your hourly rate and instead thinking about how much benefit the customer will derive from your work and charge an amount based on that value. For example, let's assume you are a process expert and you have a new technique for producing widgets that saves your customer $1 million a year. Under value pricing, you would quantify this up front and potentially charge $800,000, since there will be $1 million saved in the first year and every year thereafter. The customer, realizing there will be another $1 million by the end of the year (and every year thereafter), sees the benefit to both sides and agrees to the price.

The problem in the nonprofit world is that it is often so hard for us to quantify a direct cost savings (or revenue increase) from our support. When there is a differential in resources, that money doesn't go to shareholders (or potentially a value-pricing consultant), but rather to increasing services in some way. The one service where you could potentially use value pricing is fund-raising, but it is generally considered unethical since donors are providing funds for services, not to have someone sell to them.

ESTIMATING

With the hourly fee you created in the last chapter and having identified your fee structure, estimating will be relatively easy. If you are using an hourly agreement, you may need to have some sense of the activities your client will need and the hours and fees for them. But more likely, your client will be setting a monthly or annual limit on total charges or hours so that estimating is minimal or none at all.

For pay-one-price engagements, you can use the average historical hours needed to complete similar activities to estimate how many hours each activity in the project will take, and you can multiply that number by the hourly rate of the person performing the activity. However, if you're just starting out with your consultancy, or even if you're a mature consultancy and you haven't been tracking your hours, estimating is much more of a guess. In this case, I suggest thinking about each distinct task in your project—consider not only who can do it but also the time it's really going to take. Don't hesitate to ask peers—most consultants are willing to share information if you aren't direct competitors.

Whenever you can, with data or just guessing, try to create packages for the most common activities that provide minimodels for estimating—this will speed your estimation greatly. Here are three examples of packages we use at Civitas Strategies:

- For our one-on-one interviews (which are used to collect qualitative data), we have found they average one hour of senior-staff time. We also know that booking the calls takes about fifteen minutes per interviewee (the sum of multiple e-mails to set and confirm the time) and is done by associate-level staff. Accordingly, when we have ten interviews for a project, I assume ten hours of senior-staff time and two and a half hours of an associate's time booking them.

- Over the years, I've found that for every hour of a presentation or facilitated meeting, the preparation time is one and a half times the delivery time and roughly another 25 percent of time for an associate to review and edit the materials. Accordingly, if I have a two-hour presentation, I assume it will take me three hours, including preparation, and an associate a half hour to support preparation. An all-day, eight-hour meeting will be twelve hours of my time with an additional two hours of an associate's time.

- I've found that every month of a project requires about one hour of miscellaneous management time by the project lead. This time isn't related to a specific outcome, but rather it is for answering the questions that come up from the client or for something that needs to be solved internally. So when we are estimating a six-month project, we add six hours of my time for management.

As you can see with these examples, we can estimate a lot faster since all we need to do it is to know one variable (like the amount of time for a webinar) and we can quickly estimate the time needed, and associated fee, for multiple people.

UNKNOWN UNKNOWNS

When you have completed your estimate of the tasks and management, there is still one step—contingency. Contingency is used a great deal in the for-profit world but rarely when working with nonprofits. I think that is a significant mistake.

Contingency is a factor that covers you for all of those things that may come up that you don't know about up front. The reality is that all the estimating we mentioned previously is based on historical activities or educated guesses. Though your estimate may be dead-on based on historical activities, in reality things may not go as planned causing your actual costs to be far higher than the estimate. And when you are held to a limit (like on a pay-one-price contract), any variability is your risk. Contingency mitigates this risk by building in a little extra time to address unforeseen activities. I've found that contingencies of 0 percent, 5 percent, or 10 percent work best. I reserve 0 percent for a very simple or short project with a client I know very well (and therefore know the risks). On the other end, I use 10 percent when I don't know the client well or if I think there could be a lot of risk (e.g., if I have to facilitate a decision with a group of very contentious leaders, there's a high chance they will need more sessions and effort).

If you go with a contingency, just multiply the fee for the project by 105 percent or 110 percent (for a 5 percent or 10 percent contingency, respectively).

$$\$50,000 \times 1.10 = \$55,000 \text{ project}$$

BE HONEST, AND AVOID THE THREE TEMPTATIONS

Estimating is pretty straightforward, and if you stick to the methods mentioned here, it usually works well.

But at times the cost will be too high for a potential client. I've found this to be especially true when working for nonprofits, which are often running on very lean budgets. In those cases, you need to be honest and try to find a project that you can do that will provide value but will also have a total estimated cost your clients can afford. When you are honest about what they can buy, it always works out well, even if you don't get the project, since everyone was up front about their needs and constraints.

When clients do have, or you think they may have, price issues, the worst thing you can do is succumb to what I call the "three temptations": creating a loss leader, cutting hours while not reducing scope, or lowering your fee per hour. Despite the dangers of the temptations, I regularly hear or know of consultants engaging in them—and regretting it later.

Temptation 1: Loss Leader

The loss leader is a strategy you have experienced in your life—you get the initial product or service at a very heavy discount or free for a time, and then the prices rise up to "normal" levels. For example, television providers—cable, satellite, and the like—use this. You start out with the premium package and a low price, and then three months later, you are paying the equivalent of a mortgage payment!

The strategy is not without merit—the low initial price reduces the risk to the buyer, who then experiences your service, experiences the value, and is then more willing to pay full price. Though it is a valid pricing strategy, I have never seen it work well in nonprofit consulting. Instead of the price jumping up and everyone being happy, nonprofit customers become entrenched in the discounted price and resist increases (up to the point of ending the relationship). Around 95 percent of the time, I've seen the loss-leader strategy used in the nonprofit world, where the customer ends up having a discounted price ad infinitum. This resistance occurs even when the client is warned ahead of time about a discount. Accordingly, I avoid the loss leader—the chance to get in through an initial low price isn't worth the future tumult or lost profits.

Temptation 2: Cutting Hours

Cutting hours, the second temptation, often happens when your prospective customer can't hit your estimated cost. For example, you develop a budget that is $25,000 in total, but your client can only pay $20,000. You should go back and cut scope, but many people instead revise the hours, reducing them until they are at $20,000. The problem you have now created is twofold. First, you now have too few hours assigned to the project, and when you track through your system, it will be difficult to know if you are on target or not. Second, you have effectively discounted your costs. Similar to the loss leader, once clients get your services at a lower rate, they rarely, if ever, go back to the "real" rate, especially in the nonprofit world. Also, you may finish the project but either lose profit or compromise on quality. This could negatively affect your chances of gaining repeat or referral business from that client.

Temptation 3: Discounting

Many times, faced with a budget that is higher than a client is willing to pay, instead of cutting hours, consultants will discount their rates. In the previous scenario, the consultant would discount the project rates by 20 percent, moving it from $25,000 to $20,000. Your hours are now the same for tracking, but you still have caused two problems for yourself. First, your rate is now lower—when you built that rate, you included some profit to mitigate risk. Now, if anything goes awry, you may have a greatly reduced profit or even a loss. In my experience, about half the time you discount, you will end with a loss, so this is a very real risk.

Second, you again have reduced the costs of your services and will likely have to keep them artificially low (and accept the risks) through the life of your relationship with this customer. Worse yet (and this is true of cutting your hours as well), this discount can inadvertently flow to other customers. Here's what I mean—in the next chapter, we'll talk about the Bull's-eye and how referrals are your best strategy for sales and marketing. What often happens with referrals, especially because of the tight margins in the nonprofit world, is that when customers refer you, they will also share your pricing. Now the new prospective customer will expect services at the same cost! Before you know it, your entire rate structure has been lowered.

EXERCISE ELEVEN: PREPARING FOR CREEP AND THE TEMPTATIONS

When I talk with consultants, they often worry about how they are estimating and their accuracy. It is important to carefully estimate, but when I see project costs (and often the profitability of the entire enterprise) go awry, it is most likely related to scope creep and the three temptations. I'd like you to spend thirty to sixty minutes in a place where you are not distracted so you can prepare for the inevitable—when you are confronted by scope creep or one of the three temptations. Even if you are a seasoned consultant, you are at risk, so I suggest that you complete this exercise too. You can also do this exercise with a critical friend as well and have him or her provide feedback on your responses.

- **Step One: Focus on an Example**—Think about a time in your work, in any position or as a consultant, when you were faced with scope creep or a temptation. If you haven't experienced it, think about when it might come up in your work as a consultant. Think through the example in detail. Not just the idea of it, but when it started (even if only hypothetically) and when you realized it was a problem.
- **Step Two: Respond**—Now write out your response to the challenge—and you have to say no. This can't be a case where you accept it, but rather push back, gently but firmly. Write down how you
  - o prepare for the conversation;
  - o explain the issue (what evidence that you point to); and
  - o respond if there is any pushback.
- **Step Three: Refine**—After a day or two, review your responses in step two. Is there any way you can refine them to be even more effective?
  The final responses you end up with should be kept for later use. It can be on your cloud drive or in a notebook—you don't need them framed on your desk. But you do want to have them for when you next face scope creep and the three temptations so that when you are potentially very emotional, your notes can serve as a dispassionate approach to confronting the challenge.

7

Finding Your First Customer

There's an expression in consulting: you kill what you eat. It is a bit morbid, but it is apt. Sales are your vehicle to social impact. If you are working with nonprofits, your practice is about more than money—it is about advancing progress on causes you care deeply about. That doesn't happen when you are sitting in an office alone; it happens when you influence the organizations that are doing good work in the field. Accordingly, creating a pipeline of clients is crucial to your success as a business and in advancing the social impact you want to affect in the world.

While sales and marketing are crucial functions, most consultancies for non-profits, even ones considered medium sized in the field, lack specialized business-development or sales staff. Instead, sales and marketing rely on you and the principals of the firm. You are the one who has to go out and kill what you eat. Having to go out and sell is probably one of the most intimidating jobs you have in your firm, especially for consultants in the nonprofit world who usually lack experience in the area.

Let's start building your pipeline at the very beginning—acquiring your first customer—and move to a continuous system.

THE FIRST ONES IN THE DOOR

The greatest barrier to gaining momentum in your earliest months as a consultant is getting your first few clients. You can talk about what you did before you had your firm, but the confidence of prospective clients is gained the fastest when they know someone else has engaged you and that you have completed projects in your new venture. Ideally, to start gaining momentum, you want more than one client in your opening months—for the consultant starting solo, try for at least five clients in the first six months, even if some are entirely pro bono (more about that follows).

Getting your first customers will either be the easiest or the hardest thing you will do. Almost every time, your first customers are people or organizations that already know you well. They highly value your work and already know it—there's no need to sell them, because they are ready to invest. Typically, they are a

- current employer who knows that you want to serve others but also recognizes the need to engage you further;
- partner organization you collaborated with in a previous role; or
- person you worked for or with in the past who is at a different organization.

For some of you, you may have these customers, but you may need to broach the subject of them engaging you—I strongly encourage you to do it. The worst thing they are going to do is say no. And if you can't sell to those closest to you, it will be near impossible to sell to those you don't know at all.

EXERCISE TWELVE: FINDING CUSTOMERS QUICKLY

For some of you, your first clients may be obvious; for others, much less so. This exercise can be done in about thirty minutes almost anywhere and can help you hone in on a short list of prospects. Note that the method works any time in your business's life, so if you are ever looking to boost your clientele, this same method can help.

- **Step One: Create a List**—Create four columns, and add the headers "Name," "Reason," "Responsibility," and "Resources" atop each column, respectively. Under "Name," add anyone who significantly benefited from your help or services in the last three years. These may be customers, consumers, partners, funders, or anyone else who fits the bill. By "significantly," I usually suggest that you have measurably increased their impact, service levels, efficiency, or revenues.
- **Step Two: Identify the Prospective Customers**—Add a check box next to those you suspect have the following:
  - **Reason**—a need for your support right now or in the near future, even if they may not fully realize it themselves
  - **Responsibility**—the authority to engage consultants
  - **Resources**—the time and money necessary to engage you

  Any names with all three checked are your prospective customers. Assuming you have a number of prospects, prioritize them by the fastest potential conversion to sale, even if the sale itself may be small. Remember, if you are just starting out, you want a number of clients to show that you are in demand—the faster you sign, the better. If you are an established consultant and are here trying to boost your pipeline, the same prioritization holds since you want to keep revenue flowing into the firm, so the shorter the path to a sale, the better.
- **Step Three: Engage Them**—Reach out to your prospective customers in priority order. Start with an e-mail or call, and set a dedicated time to talk by telephone or in person. When you speak with them, ask about their needs and challenges, pivot into ways to solve them (generically, without necessarily saying anything about your firm), and then suggest that you write up a scope of work (just stating how you would solve their problem and holding off on pricing until you both agree to the scope of the project).

I know from past experience that the third step may be difficult for you, so here is a snippet of a recent conversation with a then prospective (and later actual) client to show you how it can be done. (Note that I've changed details to protect confidentiality.)

Me: I hear your challenge—your project team has five different nonprofit agencies all working together in the same school. The collaboration is making some gains, but not as much as is needed. You suspect they are collaborating well on some things and not others, but it isn't quite clear whether they are working effectively or not and how to improve their collaboration.

Prospective client: That's exactly it. I don't know where to start because I am their funder, and every time I ask, they all say everything is perfect.

Me: I think it would be helpful if you had an intermediary take a look; someone from the outside who has no stake directly in the project. That person could speak individually with the executive director and project manager for each one of the nonprofit partners as well as the key school leadership. With all these perspectives and their candid input, the intermediary could provide an assessment on implementation and suggestions on how to improve the effectiveness of the team over time. Does that resonate with you?

Prospective client: I can see how that would help.

Me: Anything you would add or delete?

Prospective client: I think our staff would also need to weigh in—I suspect some of the staff working directly with the nonprofits would have some insights as well.

Me: So if we added one-on-one conversations with your staff, that would give the analysis an even better base of information?

Prospective client: That's right! I think this process could really get us moving on the right track.

Me: Why don't I do this as a next step—I can write up a scope of work for the process we just discussed. It would include what we would do, the resulting products, and the time frame it would take us to do it. We can go back and forth as needed to refine the scope until we agree to it. And then I could cost it out, and you could make a decision. Would that be helpful?

Prospective client: That would be perfect. When could I see the scope?

This conversation is more typical than not—by focusing on customer needs and your solution, the customer can clearly hear how investing in your services will have value.

I have two last thoughts on your first clients. First, no matter how hard it may be to gain momentum, don't succumb to the three temptations. They will be tempting (pun intended), but you need to avoid them for all the reasons I discussed previously.

A few years ago, my pipeline clogged up. There were sales in the pipeline, but they weren't converting. They weren't going away either, just dragging along, not making much progress. I did exercise twelve and reached out to a former client. She had a project for which we could definitely be of service, but it was going to be risky in terms of how much time it may actually take. Against my own advice, I did lower the price to have the satisfaction of selling something, even a small project. Ironically, within forty-eight hours of signing, my pipeline started moving, and I was soon closing a number of the deals I was waiting on. The small project ended up being what I feared—taking much more time than anticipated and certainly more than I budgeted. Of course, I kept our commitment to produce the highest-quality work possible, but it certainly led to a very stressful time—and a loss in profit. Learn from my mistake—if you start to panic, stick to the system. Do exercise twelve, and work as best you can to avoid the three temptations.

Second, if you go through the exercise and still cannot come up with any prospects that have the three Rs (reason, responsibility, and resources), consider a pro-bono project. There are many nonprofits that, no matter how inexpensive your rates are, cannot afford your help. Through your existing network or finding potential pro-bono requests through LinkedIn or Idealist.org searches, start to reach out to those who may benefit from your services without charge.

Treat every pro-bono engagement exactly as you would a paying client—this is a very important point. Draft a proposal—yes the cost is zero, but this outlines the scope that you're both agreeing to, which will manage expectations. Execute the project exactly as you would for a client, with regular check-ins and high-quality reports. At the end of the project, do a closeout meeting just as you would for any client. If you end up getting other paid clients while you are working pro bono, continue to honor the commitment to the project until it is completed.

I'm being so specific about this pro-bono work because very often it is treated like a throwaway project that is done only when it's needed. If you manage this project like any other, you're creating a potential referral source just like any other, a reference that paid clients can call about your work, and, generally, good will. And, this client's executive director could easily move on to a larger organization that one day *will* be able to pay for your services. These are things you always want to build up whenever possible—from the start and throughout your consulting career.

Whatever you do to get your first clients or reinvigorate your leads, don't succumb to the three temptations.

8

Creating a Customer Pipeline

Your idea becomes a business with your first customer and stays a business with every subsequent customer. In the previous chapter, you navigated getting your clients in the door—now we have to keep them coming in.

If you are a seasoned consultant, you will most likely also need to build a pipeline. You probably already experience the ebb and flow of signing contracts that makes you worry about survival in the lean times and want to cry for mercy when too many sales convert at the same time.

Creating a pipeline is no mean feat—the number of prospects you need and the time to convert sales all conspire against you. At the same time, there is no reason not to take action. The methods in this chapter are by no means foolproof, but if implemented they will mitigate much of the effects of the peaks and valleys and build a pipeline of customers at various stages of sale, from initial contact to very close to signing.

Let's dive in.

HOW BIG IS THE BREADBOX?

To start, I want you to create an overall target for the number of leads you need for a robust pipeline. To do this, we will need to generate a few key numbers—conversation rate, average sale, average time to conversion, and estimated revenue for the year. For those of you just starting out, you will be guessing on these, but I still believe it's important to set goals and have some assumptions. Regardless, here are the key numbers:

- **Conversation rate** is how many prospective clients, on average, purchase your services. Not every sale will be made, so this gives us an idea of how many leads you need for every one successful sale. For example, you make ten "sales pitches" and, on average, secure two projects (i.e., a 20 percent conversation rate).

- **Average sale** is seemingly easy—you total all your sales in the past year (or two) by dollar value and divide them by the number of customers.
- **Average time to conversion** is the time, in months, from when you first had contact with a customer to the time you signed a contract, divided by the total number of customers. This number only includes the projects you sold, not the ones lost.
- **Estimated revenue** is how much money you will need to bring in to pay personnel, overhead, and other expenses.

With these numbers, you can calculate how many prospects you need and how long it will take to secure them. The next exercise will help you calculate values for your firm for these variables and also take you through turning this data into information that can drive your sales and marketing.

EXERCISE THIRTEEN: CREATING YOUR PROSPECT TARGET

Now I want you to create your own target numbers for sales. For this exercise, you need to sit at your computer so you can have a spreadsheet handy and pull up data as needed. There are a lot of steps, but they should move quickly—give yourself about sixty to ninety minutes to do this exercise.

- **Step One: Calculate Your Average Conversion Rate**—The conversation rate tells you how many leads, from the time of initial contact, become customers. With the conversion rate, you now know how many people, on average, need to come in the door to make one sale.

  Calculating the conversion rate itself is just dividing the number of sales (contracts you signed) by the total number of leads (the number of prospects overall).

  total number of signed contracts ÷ total number of prospects = average conversion rate

  The trick is getting the data. If you are currently consulting and can track your data (or easily find it), just pull the data for the last year or two. Be honest with yourself here—even include the leads that dropped off after one call. You need all the data.

  If you are new to consulting or can't easily collect your data, I've found that the typical conversion rate for consultancies serving nonprofit organizations is 25 percent (i.e., one in four leads becomes a sale). If you are unsure, use this number as a starting point.

- **Step Two: Calculate Your Average Sale**—This is a seemly easy number to generate—just divide your total sales for one year by the total number of projects. However, there are complexities for the new and seasoned consultant.

  If you are new to consulting, ask around to find out what a typical charge is for similar projects. Chances are if you ask a few critical friends you can find out—and the greatest probability is that you already have some idea from being in the field or through your conversations in section one (with people for whom you generated value).

If you are already consulting, you have two additional questions to be aware of as you calculate your average sale:

○   What qualifies as a sale? I'll talk about this in more detail later in the book. Having a client relationship that continues through multiple projects should be a key goal of your sales and marketing efforts. But this then leads to the question, "When does one sale to such a client end and another begin?"

I suggest you include every individual renewal (e.g., they had a one-year project with you, it ended, and they renewed for another year) or new project with an existing client (e.g., you are working with the executive director on a board-governance issue, and now she asks for a separate project to assess one a program), but not expansions (e.g., you were already doing an evaluation, but everyone agrees the sample size needs to be larger, driving up the price).

I suggest this since renewals and new projects, even with an existing client, take time to sell, just like any other client. They will probably be a shorter time to sale, and an easier one since they know you, but it is still a sale. In contrast, expanding a grant may take some effort, but it is usually an organic change based on the way the project is implemented, rather than addressing a whole separate issue.

○   How do you address services and products of different sale sizes? Some of you will have products and services that sell at similar levels, but others of you may have projects of varying sizes. For example, at Civitas Strategies, we have some services that are designed to be very short in duration (e.g., grant proposal development), whereas others are always long engagements (e.g., summative and formative evaluations). If this is the case for you, you'll want to consider performing the average-sale calculation by product or service so you can have a sense of the timing for each one.

•   **Step Three: Calculate Your Average Time to Conversion**—This is done by taking the total time, in months, of first contact with a customer to when you signed the contract and dividing it by the total number of customers. This calculation only includes "wins"—sales you converted. Plot out a year or two of data in a table or quickly on a graph to eliminate any extreme outliers (like the rare project where they talked to you two years ago, dropped off, and then suddenly reappeared and signed). For those of you just starting, I've found that it takes about six to nine months for a lead to turn into a contract in the nonprofit world (i.e., from when you first see the contract to when you sign it), so use a number in this range as an estimate.

- **Step Four: Calculate Your Estimated Revenue**—How much money will you need to bring in to pay personnel, overhead, and other expenses? This could be from your annual budget, if you have one, or the total of all your costs (your salary and other compensation, employee salaries, contractors, overhead, profit, etc.). The result is how much you need to bring in over the upcoming year.

- **Step Five: Calculate the Approximate Number of Sales You Need This Year**—Take the total estimated revenue you have for the year, and divide it by your average sale. The resulting number is an estimate of how many contracts you're going to need to sell to meet your revenue goal.

   As mentioned previously, some of you with services and products that have varying costs may want to assign revenue targets for each product or service prorated on how well they sell. For example, if a given service is your mainstay, you may want to assign 75 percent of the revenue target to that one, and then a lower-selling product gets the remaining 25 percent. In this case, divide each revenue target by the respective average sale price to get an objective for each product or service.

- **Step Six: Calculate Your Target Leads**—Now that you have the total number of projects you need to sell, multiply this number by the average conversion rate to calculate how many leads you need to have throughout the year. In other words, if only one out of every four leads becomes a project, on average, you will need four times as many leads as projects.

- **Step Seven: Set Your Quarterly Objectives**—Your average time to conversion can add another dimension to your target by letting you know how much time you need to have leads in play to make your revenue goals. Create quarterly targets for leads. To do this, divide your total target leads by four, and assign them to quarters based on your average time to conversion. For almost all of you, this will mean that you need to start selling for the next year in the current year (e.g., if it takes you four months to convert a lead to sale, the sales for the first quarter of 2025 need to start moving in 2024). This is very important to note because it affects your cash flow, annual revenue, and survival. But knowing this fact allows you to plan your work more evenly, not only in terms of sales and marketing but also in performing the project work.

Let's run through an example, since this is an important and complex series of calculations. Let's assume your calculations were as follows:

- **Conversation rate:** One in three leads
- **Average sale:** $25,000
- **Average time to conversion:** Seven months
- **Estimated revenue:** $500,000

Based on your revenue (i.e., $500,000) and your average sale (i.e., $25,000 per project), you will need to sell twenty projects in a year.

Based on the conversion rate (i.e., one in three leads), you need a target of sixty leads throughout the year.

But you can't have all sixty leads in the last month of the year and make revenue. Accordingly, you will want to set an objective of fifteen leads per quarter. Since the average time to conversion is seven months, you will want to start collecting leads for the next year as early as May of the preceding year.

HITTING THE BULL'S-EYE

Now we know how many leads you need to generate each year. Even for those of you who are consultants right now, that number may be intimidating, especially if you are used to focusing on one or two clients and are trying to grow in size. Whatever you do, don't panic.

Seeing these numbers, many consultants try to figure out how they're going to reach one thousand different organizations in every state—or something similar. As a result, they spend all their sales and marketing money on some of the plays that have the lowest chance of converting to sales.

Instead, I recommend you to focus on the Bull's-eye.

The Bull's-eye helps you prioritize your efforts on the leads that are most likely to become sales, thereby maximizing the time you invest in sales and marketing. I suggest that you do not, if tempted, just read through this section, gain the concept, and move on. Instead, use it as a tool on a regular basis to assess how you are spending your sales and marketing time. As you get a new prospect, or try to decide how to use your two hours per week on sales and marketing, plot your leads on the target, and proceed based on how close they fall to the center.

Here's the landscape of the Bull's-eye. At the heart of it are the customers, past and present, who already know and value your work. This is the quick turnaround; the fertile ground on which you can build your business. You don't need to work as hard to sell them because they've already been sold on you. These sales are not only easier; they are typically faster—instead of a six- to nine-month conversion, you'll find leads in the center of the Bull's-eye turning into sales within weeks or even days.

The second ring contains your referrals—leads generated by those who have already engaged you in the past. Sometimes these are spontaneous—the CEO of the YMCA where you worked four years ago refers you to a counterpart in another city. They can also be generated—by keeping in touch with those people who are in the center of the Bull's-eye. Engaging them periodically in conversations to see how they're doing and reminding them of the value you provide will often prompt a suggestion of who can use your services. Referrals can also be asked for—for example, if you know that an organization is looking for a consultant like you, you may want to ask a valued customer to introduce you to the executive director of the prospective client. It isn't as strong as a spontaneous referral, but it still carries much greater weight than reaching out without any previous connection.

At the outer edge of the Bull's-eye are the cold calls—those people who don't know you. This is the most difficult space of all. You're going to have to spend significant time connecting initially with these potential clients, building trust and understanding, and then selling them a solution that will meet their needs—all along the way hoping that they don't move on or choose a firm that they know better. Accordingly, these are the leads that are going to take the greatest investment of time and are the highest risk of being lost along the way.

I often get asked how I categorize requests for proposals using the Bull's-eye. It goes the same way—if you're responding to a request for proposal from an organization that knows you, or from an organization that you were referred to, you are going to have a much stronger chance of winning the request for proposal blindly than responding to a request for proposal from an organization that's three states away and has no idea who you are.

EXERCISE FOURTEEN: USING THE BULL'S-EYE

Again, the Bull's-eye is not just an idea; it is a tool you should use on a daily basis. In this exercise, we are going to craft sales and marketing strategies that rely on the Bull's-eye to generate more leads and sales. I recommend finding some quiet space and giving yourself at least an hour to complete the exercise.

If you have staff, include them in this process—it is important for them to understand how they too can positively or negatively affect sales and, in turn, the sustainability of the organization. Though this exercise reflects a moment in time, the resulting strategies and approaches will be ones that can drive early sales generation into the future, and it will also help you understand how the Bull's-eye can be applied. This is also another exercise you should revisit annually (if not more frequently) to adjust to changes in your environment and client base.

- **Step One: Plot Your Leads**—Take the time to categorize all your leads by each ring of the Bull's-eye, as I've outlined. Take a look at the results, and ask yourself these questions:
  - Is there anyone else who has the resources, responsibility, and reason to potentially hire you who also fits into those two innermost rings? Every time you add a new lead to the two center rings, remove one that sits in the outer ring. This shifts your sales and marketing activities to the area of greatest return on investment.
  - For all the leads in the two innermost rings, which are closest to sale? Put those that are closest to conversion at the top of your list—they should be your highest priority.
- **Step Two: Engage Current Clients**—I usually suggest that in the last quarter of a given project, you begin to think about and discuss with your client the next engagement—if it is appropriate. That last point is an important one—I never recommend selling just to sell. This is a fast way to burn a client out and lose a supporter at the center of the Bull's-eye.

  For each of your current clients, assess if there is a natural way that you can produce value for them, either through the work that you're currently doing or through something that you've never done with them before. For example, maybe you're coaching the CEO, and as you come to the conclusion of that engagement, you know that it has now generated the idea of creating a new strategic plan. You can suggest that your firm compete for it.

If you don't currently have clients, put a reminder in your to-do system to complete this exercise in four months, when it will not only be relevant but critical.

- **Step Three: Reconnect with Your Inner Ring—**Reconnect with five former clients. At the very least, send an e-mail. But if possible, find a time to catch up by phone for thirty to sixty minutes. Have at least two things you can share with them that would be of value—maybe a research report that could bolster their communications to funders, a new technology that could save them time and money, a rumor about a new grant program, or maybe a person they should connect with. Ground your "gifts" in what will be most valuable to them, even if it doesn't directly relate to your work. If you can't think of anything, send an e-mail saying that a recent conversation with another client sparked your memory of the project with them and you wanted to check in on how they are doing.

- **Step Four: Commit to an Assumed Authority Event or Activity—**The fastest way to move prospects from the outer ring inward is to meet them personally and do it through what I like to call assumed authority events. These are opportunities where you are positioned as an authority, giving you standing similar to being in the middle ring, as if someone has already vouched for you. These events can take many forms—for example, speaking to a group, being on a panel, and being a guest blogger. They all have one thing in common: another person or organization has put you up as an expert to others.

To be clear, this is different from having your own blog or webinar, where you still may lack any authority with those in the outer ring. In selecting an assumed authority event or activity, know that this is not just to make an appearance; make sure it will in some way connect you with people in your niche so you can generate leads and possible sales. There are a number of opportunities out there. For example, take a look at Early Learning Investigations—an ongoing series of webinars that connect early-learning experts worldwide (many of whom are consultants for early-learning professionals).

- **Step Five: Adopt a Clear Social-Media Strategy**—I'm of two minds about social media. First, it is increasing in use, especially as millennials assume a progressively stronger role in leading the field. At the same time, I see many consultants who spend a significant amount of time on it to no apparent end. Counting likes, friends, and followers is the means, not the end—the end (in terms of your consultancy) is how it creates leads or generates sales. E-mail, for example, is far more effective in reaching people, especially those you know. As you craft your social-media strategy, keep this litmus test in mind—will it generate leads and sales in your niche?

  At the most basic level, you and all of your principals should have your personal LinkedIn profiles up to date (more on that in section four), and your company should have a LinkedIn page, a Facebook page, and a Twitter handle—even if you are not very active, their existence alone is part of your bona fides.

  Adopt either one passive or active strategy that you implement at least four times a week, if not daily. I define a passive strategy as "careful watching"—checking your LinkedIn, Facebook, and Twitter feeds daily or at least four days a week (this watching is just a few minutes each time). This will give you a chance to find reasons to connect (such as seeing a change in job on LinkedIn or a blog post mentioned on Twitter that a former client would love) as well as the ability to keep up on major ideas in the field. An active strategy is putting content out—again at least four times a week. I suggest using a system like Hootsuite, which will allow you to post on multiple services at once and do so when it is most likely to be read by followers. Since generating content that is engaging can be so difficult, I recommend reading up on how to do it and also making about half your posts as link shares or reposts to other people's contents. This allows you to piggyback on content and also build your network by promoting others' work.

You can certainly choose more than one strategy in each of these steps, but be very cautious about it. Unless you are a larger firm, you need to balance your sales and marketing efforts with delighting clients through your active projects, so they will remain in the center of the Bull's-eye. Balance your time on both, and ensure you are creating your pipeline, but not at the expense of your existing projects or family commitments.

THE PEMBERTON METHOD, OR HOW TO SLEEP WELL AT NIGHT

Now you are generating leads that you have to convert to sales. But the sales pipeline is most often the Achilles' heel of consultancies. The typical cycle is as follows: you have a number of clients, you're very busy, and so sales and marketing slack off. Then you wake up at 3:00 a.m. one morning, realizing all the projects you have are sunsetting, so you panic and begin marketing and selling like mad. Everything else, including current clients and operations, is set aside to get new business in the door. You succumb to all three temptations, and before you know it, you're back to having so many clients at once, but you can't sell and market again. As a result, you're now the Hamster archetype described in the introduction. Yet there's an even darker scenario as your projects sunset—you cannot find replacements, and you soon find yourself without customers and having to close your doors.

Accordingly, it is very important to keep your sales pipeline moving. I'm not suggesting that you have to spend 100 percent of your time selling—but as a consultant, you're not just a subject-matter expert anymore, you're an entrepreneur. Even if you have other staff helping you sell, as the owner and principal, sales always rest heavily on your shoulders because you are in large part what the customer is buying. Your company's value is your expertise, reputation, and wisdom.

This is why it is crucial to always be closing to some degree—and have a reasonable pipeline of projects. So how do you manage this?

Over the years I've used a number of methods, but the one that I found most useful consistently is what I call the Pemberton Method after Dr. Don Pemberton of the University of Florida's Lastinger Center for Learning. Don introduced me to his method, converted me into an evangelist of it, and is one of the best salespeople I know. In a scant twelve years, Don was able to take an operation that consisted of himself and an assistant and move it into a global education innovation hub with a portfolio of over $24 million in projects. He has been so successful because he understands what his clients need, can deliver effective solutions, and always keeps his eye on moving sales forward.

In the Pemberton Method, you take each of your leads and outline the organization it is with, your prospective customer, the last step, and the next step (with due date, who has the action on your team, and an estimate of the total project sale). Refer to the table later in this section for a better understanding of each of these categories.

You also assign a stage of the sale. You can use any that you want, but I usually recommend five stages to my clients: lead, project design and conversations, proposal submitted, oral agreement, and win (if at any time the sale ends in a loss, take it off). You also need to assign a weight for each of the categories that reflects your data on the chance of converting a sale from that point forward. When in doubt, I suggest the weights we use at Civitas Strategies:

- Lead: 10 percent
- Project design and conversations: 25 percent
- Proposal submitted: 70 percent
- Oral agreement: 90 percent
- Win: 100 percent

The weights adjust the estimated sale value. For example, in the $5 million project I mentioned, you would put $500,000 in the last column (i.e., 10 percent of $5 million). The result is that you have a more realistic view of your pipeline value. You can quickly have an idea if you are on track to cover costs or need to generate more leads. You'll see many ways to manage a pipeline, but one of the things I really like about the Pemberton Method is that I've seen these percentages work again and again at estimating how much work you will have. Without them, I've found consultancies overestimate the value of their pipeline, since there is no reduction of value because of the stage it is in. Their mistake is that a $5 million deal that is a lead and a long shot is treated the same as the $10,000 project in proposal stage. I've found that the result of having just total numbers is complacency and ultimately a slacking on selling. (Why not? You have more than $5 million in sales coming!)

Org/Customer	Last Step	Next Step	Stage	Target Sale	Adjusted Sale (based on Stage)
H.R. Puffenstuff Living Island Foundation	Introductory call last week	Send examples of reports by Friday	Lead (10%)	$50,000	$5,000
B. Keeshan Kangaroo Community Org.	Sent proposal yesterday	Circle back in two weeks	Proposal submitted (70%)	$25,000	$17,500
M. Freeman Instit. For Easy Reading	Received oral go-ahead today	Reach out to purchasing tomorrow	Oral Agreement (90%)	$34,000	$30,600
TOTALS				$109,000	$53,100

More importantly, you have a simple system for seeing where you need to apply your time and how you need to move the various leads in the process. You'll find that, for most of you, this is far easier to manage and use than other more complex sales systems, like SalesForce.

Here's an example of how the Pemberton Method can look.

In this case, you have three prospects. Your largest opportunity is still a lead, so you only count 10 percent of the value (i.e., $5,000). Your other two prospects are much further along in the sales process, so they have a higher value (i.e., $17,500 and $30,600, respectively). Based on the Pemberton Method, you can plan a pipeline value of $53,100.

You'll find that over time you'll learn more about your pipeline dynamics. Adjust your system based on your experiences. For Civitas Strategies, we only use three categories and different weights, which reflect our experience. The result is that over time, we have a sharper and sharper picture of pipeline value and how we need to move leads to sale.

Section III: Get Help

You have made tremendous progress—you've gone from your initial idea to creating your own consultancy to getting your first clients to expanding that base into a pipeline of customers. But at some point, you're going to hit capacity.

That may be all right for you. You don't have to grow. There is a predominant belief in business in general that you need to constantly "grow or die" (e.g., as much as I enjoy Ram Charan's writings, he fervently holds this belief). If you are comfortable at full capacity, then continue on your course. That's exactly what I did in the first two years after I founded Civitas Strategies. I had spent a lot of time managing and supervising over the years, and I wanted to explore a model that was just me and a robot office. If you continue using the methods outlined in sections one and two, you can maintain your consultancy at a level that is comfortable for you.

But after those two years, I wanted to take on more work—at levels beyond what I could personally do. And for most of you, at some point you will want to continue growing to serve more organizations and have even greater social impact. (And make even greater profits—as I've said before, there is nothing wrong with that!) At the very least, you may want help to take some of the work off your shoulders.

In this next section, I will help you with this next phase in your firm's development—getting help so you can keep growing. I'll start by presenting how to decide what kind of help you need and if you are ready to bring on more people. This is never an easy decision to make, especially since as a consultant we kill what we eat, so taking on other mouths to feed is an opportunity and a risk. Accordingly, my philosophy around adding resources is to do it in the leanest way possible. That means you don't add a ton of staff. Don't have a ton of senior people, but instead figure out ways to use the lowest "cost resource"—human or otherwise—to get things done.

Once you make the decision to move forward, you'll need help in finding and using your new resources, so I will also cover how to recruit, train using an observational approach, and delegate to your team. I'll conclude by looking at ways for you to cost-effectively develop your staff.

9

The "When" and "What" of Adding Resources

Let me start this chapter with the potentially disappointing, but nonetheless true, statement: there's no easy way to decide when you're ready to add people. It is much more of an art and roll of the dice than it is a science. In consulting, you kill what you eat, and it's hard to know how much food you're going to have that far into the future. And as we all know, even if you're doing well one day, things can change. That's why at some point you need to take a leap of faith—and in this chapter I'll show you how to make it an educated leap of faith.

To ensure that they are ready to add staff, I counsel clients to think about how they can automate first, contract second, and hire staff with the lowest skill level possible third. This approach will limit the expansion of your costs in the near and long term as much as possible.

The question to add resources typically starts because you or one of your team become swamped over time or you see an impending tsunami (e.g., the big contract that is in the final stages of approval and will require the time of three extra staff members). The usual reaction to both situations is to panic and start hiring. However, this is exactly what you do not want to do. Whatever resource you add—whether it's subscription to a new technology, a contractor, or certainly a new staff member—is a cost that will definitely affect your bottom line and may be one that you will have for a while.

Before we get started, I want to talk about the forms your human resources can take: contractors or employees. Many consultants don't really understand the difference and basically treat anyone part time as a contractor and anyone full time as an employee. In truth, that's not the difference, and the IRS and state taxation agencies are cracking down on firms that use contractors who should be employees. Knowing the difference is important, but at the same time, there are few hard-and-fast rules—check with your lawyer or tax professional.

But I will provide a quick overview for reference.

Basically, there is no simple litmus test for determining if someone is a contractor or an employee. Instead, the IRS looks at three categories:

1. **Behavioral**—How much control does the company (vs. person/contractor/employee) have over the position? For example, does your company set the requirements around the hours of work, what equipment or tools need to be used, or the training needed? (If yes, then this person is an employee.)
2. **Financial**—How is the person paid by the firm? For example, is the person paid every week for a set number of hours (employee), or does the work vary (contractor)? Do they have regular expenses that are reimbursed (employee)?
3. **Type of Relationship**—Does the person work on a contractual basis or on short-duration projects (contractor)? Does the person have other clients (contractor), or is your firm the one and only (employee)?

Again, these questions are not easy to answer, but usually the advice professionals give is, if it walks like a duck and talks like a duck, it's a duck. In other words, if they act as employees would in their position, and in their relationship with the firm, then they are probably employees. But again, I strongly urge you to seek competent counsel or contact the IRS for determination.

DO I NEED HELP?

As mentioned previously, your decision about whether you need help or not will probably be when you're most stressed because you're already overwhelmed or feel like you are about to be. Though your fight-or-flight reflex will be engaged, I always suggest that clients take a deep breath and take a two-phase approach to assess if and what resources they need:

*   **Phase One: Task Analysis**—Before you do anything, you need to know how current resources are being used and the resources you will need to meet the demands of a new project. I suggest you do this by inventorying tasks and then grouping them by similar skill level and duration.

- **Phase Two: Identify Resources**—I suggest using some simple questions to determine the level of resources you really need based on the tasks identified in phase one.

Let's explore each of the phases in kind.

PHASE ONE: TASK ANALYSIS

If you suspect it is time to add resources, there are two easy ways to inventory your tasks ahead of analysis. If you find yourself suddenly swamped or if you are just feeling like you are at risk of being swamped, start with a time study. Though they are rarely used by consultants for nonprofits or even nonprofit leaders themselves, I'm a very big fan of time studies. The main argument I hear against them is that people think they will be intrusive and difficult. But you don't need to do them for an incredibly long time, and every time I have had clients do them, even when they have been resistant and said they weren't necessary, they've come back to me with appreciation because they had an even keener understanding of what their needs really were.

For example, I recently had a client who was overwhelmed with work on her contracts. She knew it was too much for her and was considering bringing on a midlevel consultant but didn't have the funds to do so. At the same time, the work continued—she had become a Hamster. I convinced her to do a time study first. Just two business days' worth of data that we could review. The analysis revealed a pretty common issue—a startling amount of her time was dedicated to scheduling meetings and calls and rescheduling them and to minor e-mails—about 25–38 percent of the day in total. These are all things that could be automated or performed by someone at an administrative level. I've seen this one change free up one to three hours a day for senior-level consultants. Instead of hiring for a more expensive position, she committed to some new technology and a part-time administrative assistant.

For many of you, the drive to add resources may be due to a rapid expansion—like the new project you just secured that will double your work. This may seem like a far-fetched scenario, but about half the consultancies serving nonprofits that I have worked with have experienced a similar period of growth. In cases such as this, I recommend dissecting the scope to identify all the tasks you'll need to complete the project.

Regardless of whether you do a time study or a review of the project scope, you are going to want to group the identified tasks by skill level and duration (i.e., how long you will need the support).

EXERCISE FIFTEEN: TASK ANALYSIS

The time it will take depends on your needs. If you're conducting a time study, it will be implemented over two to three days. If you're dissecting scope, that will probably be an hour to two and should include any members of your team who will be working on the project (even outside consultants). The analysis of either can happen very quickly after completion and should take less than an hour.

- **Step One: Collect Data**—As mentioned previously, you'll want to collect data differently, depending on the need.
  - **If you or a team member are now overloaded because of a number of different projects, do a time study**—Before starting the study, you should create a table or spreadsheet with the day marked in fifteen-minute increments. Don't worry about making it pretty; just make sure you have enough room to quickly jot down what you are doing in each increment.

    Simply log what you do in the fifteen-minute increments. This is for your use, so be honest with yourself—were you really writing, or were you checking out the latest posts on Facebook? If you are working on the same thing, again feel free to use a line or ditto marks to indicate a block of time. In the large block of time, try to note why it was so long, if it may not be obvious. For example, "writing but kept getting calls." For activities lasting fewer than fifteen minutes, try to be specific about each activity. An entry might read, "got coffee, checked e-mail, and returned to editing doc."

    Identify the tasks that are ones that need to stay with you no matter what (e.g., reviewing and approving payroll) versus those that could theoretically go to others (e.g., scheduling phone calls and interviews). Put those taking the most time and needing the least skills at the top. An example of what could end up on the top of the list is making travel arrangements. Consultants often travel, and though booking travel doesn't necessarily need a very high skill level, it can take up a significant amount of time.
  - **If you are going to have significant, rapid growth due to a new or pending project, dissect the scope**—Start by taking your scope for the

new project and identifying all the tasks involved. This is more art than science. Start with the highest levels, and then move to greater detail. For example, if you have a three-part project to collect data, analyze it, and write up and present the results, those three buckets would be your starting point. Then, as you go into more detail on each bucket, keep making it more granular. The report for the project may have tasks for writing, editing, and final review.

- **Step Two: Analyze the Results**—It is ideal to have someone else look at the results and provide an interpretation. It is easy to miss the forest for the trees, but worst case, you can do it yourself. Start by putting the tasks on sticky notes, since you can easily move them around to group or reconfigure the tasks. Set aside any tasks that you cannot let go of—I usually use the litmus test of ones that will make or break client relationships. Be judicious with the ones you set aside. Sometimes it can be tempting to think that everything needs to start and end with your own efforts.

Next, you want to categorize each task along two dimensions. First, the skill level of the task. This will depend on how deep your organization is, but for most of you, the division could be senior, midlevel, entry level/administrative, and automation. The second dimension is the duration over which the task will be executed. Is this a one-time task needed for a set period or something we need to do on an ongoing basis throughout the life of the project? The second variable helps you know how much of a commitment you need to make to the use of a new resource.

The result will be, visually, where you need to be able to add resources by the level of skill and duration.

Here's an example of how the exercise can play out. Let's assume your analysis came up with the following tasks:

- creating and tracking client invoices
- conducting client-coaching calls
- scheduling and confirming coaching calls
- speaking at major events to sell your services
- preparing your company tax return

You opt to put aside "speaking at major events to sell your services," since the conferences that you attend really only want you (as opposed to others who may be on your team).

You plot them and come up with the following:

One Time:
- ❍ Preparing your company tax return (midlevel)

Ongoing:
- ❍ Conducting client-coaching calls (senior level)
- ❍ Scheduling and confirming calls (entry level/admin)
- ❍ Creating and tracking client invoices (automation)

Only one, "preparing your company tax return," is not ongoing—it is once a year—due to some complexities of your business, you'll need a somewhat experienced accountant. That leaves three ongoing tasks. Coaching is your main service, and you'll need experienced staff if they are to take on some of your clients. In contrast, an administrative employee could do the scheduling of calls. Developing and tracking your invoices can be automated using FreshBooks or a similar system.

PHASE TWO: IDENTIFY RESOURCES

Now that you know which tasks you need to delegate, we can look at how you decide on the type of resource to engage. This is often a tough process for most consultant entrepreneurs, especially those who serve nonprofits. There is a tendency to want to make this decision a binary one—you either hire somebody full time and go "all in" on a resource or don't fill any position and take on the strain of continuing the work without additional help. In truth, there are a lot of options for the resources that you can engage. You may use automation, a contractor, or even a part-time employee. The driver throughout this process needs to be your profitability. You won't serve anyone well if you take on too much and put an undue strain on your profit or take on too few resources and put undue strain on yourself and your team. Whenever possible, I suggest clients automate first, contract second, and hire third, to ensure they use their revenues as wisely as possible.

MAKING A LIST

I want you to ask yourself if you can use procedures or similar tools (such as checklists) to reduce resource needs or enable lower-skilled people to perform the work. I have always been a big fan of procedures, checklists, templates, and other tools that can help you and your team move more quickly and more efficiently. They can not only help you reduce costs, but they can also be a great way to leverage your resources by reducing the time needed to complete tasks and reducing the skill level needed to perform tasks, thereby reducing the cost of talent.

When you think about developing some of these tools, I find clients immediately go to the image of a large compendium of an organization's policies and procedures, which would be overwhelming for any small enterprise. I want you to consider them in a much more strategic and simple way. As you look over the tasks that are repetitive or those that are going to require a new hire, consider how even the simplest things, like checklists, could reduce the time or the skill level needed.

Let me provide two examples that can help you see this playing out in consultancies.

First, here's an example of how these tools can actually reduce resource need. A few years ago, we were advising a small consultancy that was having trouble around communications. It had a very small staff (fewer than five people) and wanted to do a better job of getting the word out to the media, and also to social media, about

clients and projects. I was having such a difficult time that the owner, our customer, was considering engaging an outside firm—though the cost would put a strain on the organization. I was a bit stunned, since the staff was very skilled in communication. In talking with the owner and with the other staff members, I soon realized that they were their own biggest challenge. They were able to do each of the communications tasks effectively—one was adept at writing press releases, another at writing social media posts, and then another was actually getting them out. The real problem was that nobody was clearly responsible for any piece at any time.

Without feeling any pressure or responsibility, the tasks were done ad hoc, many times too late, or they would be written and then wouldn't get posted because the person who did that function had other things on his or her plate. The staff also said that prioritizing wouldn't be a problem as long as they knew that it was a priority. In response, we crafted a simple flowchart that told each person what his or her responsibility was and to whom he or she handed his or her work product. We also had the trigger (i.e., a new project or major event) clearly articulated and designated the person on the chain who received it first. Each person in the flowchart had twenty-four hours to do his or her piece. The result was that things started to work smoothly, and they found that they had just enough people to do what they needed to do.

The second example is just about how things can be a little bit more efficient. For many years at Civitas Strategies, every time we had a new client, it was my personal responsibility to set up every project. This included creating the entry in the time-keeping system, updating QuickBooks and setting the invoice schedule, creating a file in Dropbox, developing a kickoff meeting with everyone who was going to be on the project, and on and on. Unfortunately, with the ebb and flow of work, I would never get it done all at once, but rather would do it "just in time," which is a nice way of saying only when I absolutely had to! It made things a bit choppy because sometimes we were ready to send the invoice and I had to drop everything to set the client up in the system. Or we were going to save a draft but realized a Dropbox client folder had not been set up yet. Our team ended up developing a quick procedure for setting up a new client that included everything. I still do many parts of it, but by clearly laying out what other people had to do, I was able to use less expensive resources and share the burden so it was not just resting on me. The result was a lot less pain, anxiety, and effort all around.

EXERCISE SIXTEEN: DETERMINING THE NEEDED RESOURCES

Bring your project team or management team together, or just you as the case may be, and allow for an hour or two, depending on the size of your need. Throughout, your priority should be to find resources for the tasks that are easiest to fill.

- **Step One: Low-Hanging Fruit**—Start by identifying any tasks that someone else on your team, or who you are already engaged with as a consultant, can easily take on. Many times, when you see all the tasks up on sticky notes on a wall, you get some perspective and realize this or that could be added since it is for a short time or very easy. Also consider how procedures, checklists, or other similar tools could dramatically decrease the burden of tasks.

- **Step Two: Automation**—Next, look for the things you can easily automate. I define "easily" as being able to use an online or existing system with little investment for customization. You already automated a number of functions in creating your MVC, but there are new systems arising all the time (we'll highlight them on smallbutmightybook.com) and also new needs that we didn't cover. If you aren't clear which tasks might be automated, look for those that require repetition. Chances are that they could be at least eased through technology. For example, one process I see all the time is proposals. It never ceases to amaze me how often clients will start a proposal from whole cloth, taking time to set up the cover, sections, "about us" spiel, and other parts that are used over and over again. Instead, they can easily set up a template in their word-processing software that has most of the sections that are going to be eternal and focus on just updating what they need. The result is something that is not only less time consuming but also higher quality, since you know what is going to be consistent.

- **Step Three: Specialized or Time-Limited Activities**—Look for tasks that are highly specialized or occur on a periodic basis. The former can cover a gamut of project work (e.g., a specialized financial expert you need for a cost-benefit analysis) or operations (e.g., an accountant or other professional to prepare your taxes). If the specialist is needed for the day-to-day function of your consultancy, then proceed to step four. But my guess is that most of the time when you need specialists, you won't need their full-time attention, which segues into our second category, those tasks that only come up for a fixed amount of time. Yes, they may occur multiple times in a year, but they are irregular or temporary (e.g., a burst of work that will calm down in ninety days). In both cases, you will probably want to contract with an individual or firm.

- **Step Four: Everything Else**—By now, you have knocked out all the quick and easy items and are left with tasks that will need to be completed by an employee. Before you proceed, though, look at the time and skill level needed. Make sure the time demands a full-time person. There are many people who want to work part time (e.g., a parent who has a child in school and can work earlier in the day but wants to be free starting in the midafternoon). Unless you actually have a full-time need, the part-time option will be more cost effective. Think of the skill level in a similar way. Do you need one full-time midlevel professional or one part-time administrative-level person and one part-time midlevel professional?

This last point is a crucial one—I find consultants in the nonprofit world tend to want to hire a senior-level person over a more cost-effective junior person, even though this makes sustaining the position more difficult. I believe it's because the nonprofit consulting business has tight margins with few staff, and therefore leading can be a lonely endeavor with few peers with which to collaborate. But again, you kill what you eat, so a more senior person means a bigger mouth to feed!

When you are answering any of these questions, think about how the tasks could be proceduralized. Is there any way to teach them to someone with lower skills? Can you have a checklist that a person can run through? Even if it doesn't relieve all the burden of the task, anything you can source at a lower rate will make your organization more efficient.

NOTHING IN THE WORLD IS FREE

One type of resource that you may have noticed I don't talk about is the free resource—interns or projects that local undergraduate or graduate college classes take on free of charge. It's not that I don't believe in the importance of these programs. In fact, I am proud to say that I have started three internship programs, and throughout my career I have personally mentored over fifty interns (on top of other mentoring I have done). The reason why I don't include them is that, especially for consultancies to nonprofit organizations with tight profit margins, free resources are never easy solutions.

That's because internships and college or graduate-school class assignments need to include a significant amount of learning; otherwise, you're just exploiting the student or intern. In other words, these programs are not free—instead, you pay with your time to help students or interns truly learn about the field and the work. If you're willing to take that payment on, then consider them like any other paid resource that we discussed, and set up their position as one that's going to not only create value for you but also ensure that there is going to be enough time that they truly learn and develop as professionals.

10

Lean Talent Search

After all of your work in the last chapter, you have determined that you now need to find a new resource. However, finding and developing talent is one of the greatest challenges for the nonprofit-serving consultancy. Unlike most for-profit consultancies, you're running on tight profit margins and can't offer astronomical salaries, benefit packages, and development opportunities. At the same time, you should not give up or settle for the first person you find. There are ways that you can quickly hone in on talent that will get you a reasonable pool of candidates without overwhelming you. Also, know that I recommend this process, even when you have an internal or known candidate for the position. There is always a benefit to having people compete for a position. Even if they know that the odds are in their favor, knowing that they competed for and won the position will boost their confidence, and yours in them, as the right choice.

LEAN SEARCH

Finding talent will be challenging. When you compete against for-profit firms, they can offer more money and benefits. When you look at talent in the nonprofit world, many will resist your organization as not being "mission driven" (failing to see the benefit you may have on others' missions). As a result, you need to seek out talent like a headhunter. But doing that on a shoestring budget is not easy. This challenge led my firm, Civitas Strategies, to create an approach to talent search that we call lean search. We are planning on taking the approach open source in early 2017 by distributing it via a free e-book. But I want to provide you with a preview here so you can start using it now.

In the early years of Civitas Strategies, I would never have imagined getting into talent search. In fact, for years, I actively resisted it, even when clients would ask. I believed it was a highly specialized field that involved a certain level of alchemy. However, in 2014, a client of ours needed a search performed and, appreciating and trusting us so greatly, insisted that we do it. After this process, I realized that there were opportunities to make the process more effective and efficient, so I challenged our team to develop a search model that was 50 percent less expensive and 50 percent faster than a traditional search, with an eye to having a solution for smaller, leaner organizations (we used the business model canvass, which we will talk about in section four). This service quickly became a core offering for us. In practice, we found our service is 60 percent faster and 50 percent less expensive with results that, according to our clients, were the same or exceeded a traditional search. We continued to refine the process and will start offering it as an open-source resource to anyone wanting to use it, nonprofit or for-profit. If you check the Civitas Strategies website (www.civstrat.com) starting in early 2017, you will be able to download the process contained in a free e-book.

HOW IT WORKS

Lean recruiting is based on two assumptions. First, that you will need to compete for talent and that this competition is, to some degree, stacked against you. Again, when you serve nonprofits, you can't offer grand salaries and benefits, and you probably don't have a large human-resources office to do all the work for you. Second, since you have to compete for talent, that is going to mean actively seeking out the types of people you need, rather than just placing a passive ad or asking in your network and hoping that the right person will find you.

Lean recruiting uses three steps to conduct a search: define, discover, and decide. Let's look at each in detail.

DEFINE

In step one, define, you get very clear about the job you're trying to place; it culminates in what I call the three-part job announcement, which we have found to be crucial in attracting the right talent.

Traditional position announcements rarely have any sort of excitement around them. They usually start with an all-too-brief description of the organization, then launch into the job like a tremendous laundry list. These announcements are born out of a desire to make all the internal players happy by ensuring everything they want is included. In a world where you have to compete for talent, you have already hamstrung yourself as potential talent passes on the positions because they are feeling uninspired and overwhelmed by the weight of the requirements.

Instead, I recommend our three-part job announcement, which contains the following:

- A compelling description of the organization that excites candidates and sparks a desire to be part of your team
- Limited position description and requirements that focus on what is most essential
- The fine print, which includes all the details on how to apply

More than just a document, the three-part job announcement is a process. The first section forces you to really think about what others would see as most exciting about your organization. In the second section, you front-load the difficult work of setting tight decision criteria. This is the opposite of the norm, where an organization starts with the lengthy description to narrow the candidates down and then interview the best. Then, in the deliberation process, hiring managers realize they didn't need the long list of A, B, C, D, E, and F but really only A and B and potentially D. Now they have a pool of candidates who may not fill the most urgent needs. By making the tough decisions of priorities up front, you help ensure your prospective employees can see themselves clearly in the position and be confident in applying. This also ensures that you will have the broadest pool of candidates who meet the most significant needs of the firm.

Further, I suggest that clients not only hone in on criteria but also set up a score-card. For most of my career, I didn't use more than what I like to call the Flip Method. I would flip through the applications received, and if the cover letter or résumé didn't catch my eye, I moved on. The method was a direct reaction to the huge number of résumés I would receive because of online sites and the ease of e-mailing applications. With the volume you receive, you need to cut through clutter quickly.

However, in developing lean search, we found that the latest human-resources research recommends scorecards. Once we employed them, our team at Civitas

Strategies understood why it was recommended so highly. The scorecard itself is simple—you create a basic outline with weighted scores for each of the characteristics in your job description based on what you believe is most crucial for success in the position. Sometimes people get hung up and worried about relative weights of the variables. Don't. This is more art than science. Limit yourself to one hundred points and distribute them among the characteristics so that you end up with the score of zero to one hundred.

If you use gradations, clearly state them up front. For example, instead of having a variable be "experience in public housing, up to five points," it could be "experience in public housing—fewer than three years (two points), more than three but fewer than five years (three points), and more than five years (five points)."

As each application comes in, because the scorecard is so simple, almost anyone on staff can score the application packages. When you're done, you very clearly see who rises to the top and what your trade-offs are going to be. For example, you may find the prospective employees with one key skill have not been in the field very long so you may be willing to trade off that skill for longevity.

The method, though simple, forces you and your organization to make strategic decisions about the candidates up front. There's no question later of who you were looking for. It also simplifies the initial review of applicants to a point where almost anyone can do it, and you end up with data that you can use to easily review and make decisions.

EXERCISE SEVENTEEN: BUILD A THREE-PART JOB ANNOUNCEMENT

To develop your three-part job announcement, you may want to engage your team in a meeting or, if it is just you, find a quiet place. Give yourself an hour or two, and wait at least a day before returning to do a final edit.

- **Step One: Sell the Best Organization in the World**—Draft one to three paragraphs about your organization and why an applicant would want to work there. Whenever possible, try to use not only superlatives but also names and numbers to back up the draft. Ask yourself the following:
  - What is the one reason why our organization is more attractive than many others?
  - What are the two to three clients or projects that are most compelling?
  - Which statistics of our growth or impact will motivate and excite talent?
- **Step Two: Find the Core Description, and Create a Scorecard**—You want to hone in on the key criteria that are going to be used to select the candidate, which of course must also correlate with what will make that candidate successful. Answer the following questions:
  - What are the three to five things that are absolute core requirements? If nothing else in the whole world, what will the ideal candidate have that will make him or her attractive to you and successful in the position?
  - Beyond this set, what are the next five to seven requirements?
  - Add metrics and thresholds whenever possible. For example, you don't want something that says, "understands public advocacy." Instead, be specific, such as, "has led at least two campaigns to change public policy, regardless of their success." These five to seven things should be lesser characteristics—some of the basics (e.g., the degree that they should have) or things that would be optional (e.g., a particular academic specialization).

On the first run through, you may want to start by writing all the possibilities down and then consolidating and eliminating to get to the core requirements. Try not to go past any of the limits in these questions—when you do, you start drifting into a laundry list and potential confusion.

Once you have the list, create your scorecard in a spreadsheet or similar tool. Limit yourself or your search team to one hundred points to distribute. Ensure each variable is as clear as possible.

- **Step Three: Outline How to Apply**—The last part of the description is the "how to apply" section. This part lets candidates know where they submit their information and what else you may want. For example, you may ask for a writing sample that candidates feel would be pertinent to your evaluation. Ask them to send everything to a dedicated e-mail (e.g., associateconsultant@civstrat.com) for the position. This will allow you to avoid distractions and clutter in your main e-mail inbox.

Now that you have your three-part job announcement, let's share it with the world!

DISCOVER

As you move into your search, I want you to consider the two "wheres":

1. Where will they be geographically (or maybe anywhere at all if it can be a remote position)?
2. Where will they be in their careers (not just level of decision-making but also the types of organizations [e.g., for-profit or nonprofit, large or small], credentials they may have, years of experience, and specific skills)?

The geography is rarely just national or local—I have found that it's usually somewhere in between. You want to think about geographies that have similar culture, where cost-of-living differentials are similar, or maybe about geographies that are nearby or in some way connected. For example, we do a lot of work in the state of Florida. For a variety of historical and cultural reasons, the state is connected to the New York tristate area. Also, the cost of living is significantly less in Florida, making it attractive to those in and around New York City (though jobs in Florida are likely to pay less due to the reduced cost of living, I've found the differential is, most of the time, beneficial to the job seeker). Based on these facts, when recruiting for positions in Florida, we found that cross-posting in New York, New Jersey, and Connecticut can be productive.

In terms of organizations, those that are similar or related to what you do in some cases may be a direct correlation. For example, if you work exclusively in the K-12 education environment, you may look for those who are in that area. But you may also want to consider other areas of education or even other fields, as they could have relatable skills. For example, resource-development jobs are very difficult to recruit for, especially in the education field. So you may want to look at other areas of public service that have similar challenges in raising money for something that is often a long-term benefit, such as environmental organizations.

Once you have the "two wheres" answered, the next step is to look at your strategies for distributing and pushing the job. A point to remember is that ideally you don't just want people who are unemployed and look good—instead you want to be open to all possible talent, even those who may not have considered a transition until they heard about your amazing opportunity. As a result, you want to choose distribution channels that not only get those who were trying to find a new position but also are a little bit of a headhunting exercise where you push it out to those who you would love to have on your team.

With this in mind, there are three strategies we have found to be particularly effective. (Keep in mind we tested more, but these are the ones that really get you the return on your investment):

- **Share with Your Network**—This means not only asking people in your personal network but also asking any of your team members and clients to share it. You may have some hesitation on this, but both your other team members and your clients are typically excited about growth and having the right talent to support them, so they tend to be ready partners.

- **List on One "Feeder" Job Board**—Note that I said singular "job board," not ten of them. In the era of Internet robots and search engines, if you put your listing on the right job board, it will be picked up by every other job board, usually within twenty-four to forty-eight hours, without you doing anything. We found idealist.org and Bridgespan's job boards to be particularly effective, not only in reaching the type of talent you want for a public-service consultancy but also for having your listing picked up by any other job board that potential candidates might be following. In both cases, the fees are not that high, so in just posting to one, you're also doing this in a cost-effective way.

- **Headhunt on LinkedIn and the Internet**—On the Internet-search side, you may want to use a website like GuideStar. These types of sites can help you find the types of organizations that are most directly related to your work or analogous to it. You can then find people related to your work at an organization or the types of people you may want. Similarly, on LinkedIn you can do an advanced search to find people and reach out to them either in the system or by finding their e-mail on the Internet. Reach out to them as an ally and not as a job prospect. Send a soft e-mail saying that you are looking for people like them or that they are in the types of organizations in which you'd be looking for talent. You can say that you thought that somebody in their network might be interested and ask if they would please pass it on accordingly. Of course, many of them will realize that this message is as much for them as it is their network, but that's all right. Most people are flattered that you would consider hiring them, and not insulted or hurt. And of all the projects on which we've used this method, we have yet to have people e-mail us back and say that they are deeply upset by this. Instead, they're usually happy to share it since good job opportunities are rarely seen.

As the résumés come in, you can begin to score them using your scorecard. Leave two to four weeks to accept résumés. In our digital age, applicants tend to move faster, but it can still take a while for the word to get out.

DECIDE

Now that all your candidates are scored, you can set a cutoff for who is in the decision process. I find that typically there will be an applicant "cliff" in your data—a point where the scores markedly drop off. The candidates above the cliff are usually a reasonable cohort for a decision process. However, if you don't have a great number, consider limiting your cohort to no more than ten to fifteen candidates at the start.

I recommend having two to three steps in your interview process. The first step is always a screening call. This is short, informal, and has two objectives. First, it ensures that candidates are interested in the job as it is. This means reminding them of the hours or other requirements, such as having to be on-site. Additionally, I strongly recommend sharing a salary range or, in the case of contractors, an hourly-rate range. This may feel uncomfortable, but it also isn't fair to you or to them to waste time if their expectations are far above what you are willing or able to pay. I find that about 25 percent of candidates will be removed in the screening process—either because you decide they're not a right fit or because they say that the job is not what they expected or are willing to take.

With the remaining candidates, do one or two rounds of interviews based on the quality of the remaining pool and how excited you are about them. Ideally, I have found that having a final pool of four or five candidates—whether that's in one round or two—is the most manageable. I recommend that you talk with every candidate and also engage the manager of the position and a peer, if appropriate.

So what do you ask? I strongly recommend avoiding the tried-and-true questions that focus on the things you can most easily find out—such as how many years they were at a position and if they liked it or what they have learned. Instead, I focus on behavioral questions, which give you powerful insights into candidates by asking them about scenarios that actually happened to them. This enables you to have a sense of not only their skills but also how they approach problems, how they deal with other people or clients, and if they can think on their feet.

You want to focus on behavioral questions that are extremes.

Instead of...	Ask/Say...
How did you start a recent project?	Talk to me about a project that went awry. When did you realize it? What did you do in reaction?
What are your strengths and weaknesses?	Tell me about a time when you felt most confident working with a client.
	Tell me about a recent project when you were working with a client and felt like you were clearly out of your depth.

There are many behavioral questions available to you, and you can certainly try different combinations. Choose ones that reflect the greatest stresses or challenges of your work or the places where you provide greatest value.

ALWAYS BE LOOKING

Before we transition to the intake and training of your new employee, or engage a new contractor, I want to offer one final thought. Similar to the "always be closing" concept, I recommend that you always look. Yes, you may not be ready to hire someone right now, and that person may not be ready to be hired right now. Similarly, you may run into consultants who are very interesting. You can find out more about what they do now and really understand how you might use them. You may not engage them for a year, but when it's time, you know you've hired well. It's also a great way to support your sales and marketing—you provide a natural opportunity to talk about what they value and how they generate value, and conversely how you do the same.

11

Bringing Your Team Up to Speed

" M anagement" is often a dirty word, especially in the nonprofit world—we only want to talk about "leadership" and other trappings of "being in charge." But the reality is that there is no leadership without the ability to manage. That is, whether you own a consultancy with one part-time consultant or you have one hundred employees in different locations, your ability to be an effective enterprise will be limited by your ability to work with those on your team.

Management is a vast field, and there are a lot of wonderful books about how to manage effectively. What I'd like to focus on here are three key points as you grow your consultancy:

1. What do you do when you first engage an employee or contractor?
2. How do you effectively train and enculturate a new team member?
3. How do you effectively delegate tasks?

SO NOW WHAT?

The moment you engage a new consultant or employee is very exciting. When I was in a physical office, I always loved to welcome new team members with flowers or a gift at their desk. In virtual offices, I make sure that I reach out and talk to them and tell them how excited we are to have them on the team. But as exciting as this moment is, it should also be one where you start the relationship with some formality.

I had a client a few years ago who had recently hired a new contractor. She seemed wonderful on paper and had a great reputation and wonderful references. However, the client immediately began to wonder how this woman had ever survived in the working world. She didn't hit her deadlines, the work was poor, and she took any criticism very defensively. My client opted to separate from the contractor, and when we were talking about how to handle it, she admitted that they didn't have any contract—there was no clear way to end the relationship nor to protect the things that my client's customers may want to keep in confidence and had trusted to the consultancy. The result was a very delicate dance to remove the consultant over weeks that involved lost time, lost effort, and lost money.

With this story in mind, and many others similar to it that I've witnessed over the years, I strongly recommend that you not engage anyone, consultant or employee, without some sort of written agreement. This is another place that I will urge you to get legal counsel—creating a standard employment-and-contractor agreement is relatively inexpensive and one of those things you want done correctly.

Your legal counsel can provide you with details and options, but there are a few key points that I want to highlight for you. First, you will want to have some sort of nondisclosure agreement that limits the person's ability to share what he or she learned while working with you. This is a good practice not just for your sake but also for your clients'. Many contracts I've had with clients, especially large philanthropic foundations, include clauses where I need to ensure that I won't disclose anything but also that nobody who works for me—contractor or employee—will either. So that nondisclosure clause ensures that you are keeping your word and have everything in place in case you're ever audited by a client.

Your agreement will also include some sort of noncompetition clause. I firmly believe that many noncompetition clauses can go way too far and stifle innovation and competition, and this is why many states are starting to regulate them (another reason to check in with an attorney). At the same time, your client relationships are absolutely crucial to your present and future. Remember what we learned about the Bull's-eye—your best sales and marketing opportunities are those clients who already know and value your services. Accordingly, you should have some protections about any employee or consultant assuming those relationships outside of your firm.

Finally, make sure that there is a clear section in the agreement describing the terms of separation. These terms are often forgotten—everyone works under the assumption that if things don't work out, you just part ways. However, it isn't always so clean. Having clear terms as to how you will end a contractual or employment relationship can help ensure a smooth sunset to a relationship, particularly one that is not going well, and will reduce the chance of either party leaving with hard feelings that could jeopardize the reputation of the other.

DELEGATION

In my work with other nonprofit consultancies, I have found delegation to be a consistent challenge. Whether it is the principal of the organization or his or her senior- or midlevel managers, there are consistently issues with how to delegate effectively that then lead to frustration—when products miss the mark, are not delivered on time, or lack the quality needed. This is a result of the way nonprofit consultants typically operate in the field—they are specialists in a subject matter of importance to communities, families, and children, but not necessarily experienced in managing an organization or their own time.

I found that Stephen Covey's method of delegation presented in his *Seven Habits of Highly Effective People* is a simple yet powerful way to delegate. For years I had his three main points taped to my desk at multiple jobs and companies as a constant reminder of what I needed to do to give effective direction. He recommends three things:

- **Let the person know what you want**—It is not only about the product but about what it is going to be used for and how success will be defined.
- **Let the person know when it is due**—I am very anal retentive about deadlines, and I recommend that you be too. I cannot tell you how many times customers have said that one of Civitas Strategies's greatest strengths is the fact that we deliver on time. I find it incredible that keeping commitments is a differentiator, but it is one you can easily adopt. When you give a deadline, you need to make it clear that it is firm, but not draconian. When I give deadlines to people I work with, I understand that life will come up—children will get sick, cars will get into accidents and need to be fixed, pipes will burst— these things happen and will throw people off track for deadlines. What I always ask is if you can't meet a deadline, let me know as soon as possible. That way I can make a determination if we can move the deadline and agree to a new one, if I need to redelegate it to someone else, or if I need to do it

myself. Also, I always convey that the latter two decisions are not a punishment, but rather a commitment to keep deadlines with our client and ensure things are done on time.

- **Let the person know about available resources**—These resources can be tools, files, or other things that staff can use to complete the project. Usually in consulting, your resources are going to be other people within your organization. You may question why you have to specify this, but it's very important. This goes back to the "time is money" challenge in consulting. Though teamwork is great, that time when two or three of your team members are meeting is time that they're not working on other projects, so you need to make sure that it is absolutely valuable. Accordingly, when I delegate, I usually specify something along the lines of "you should connect with Alison for an hour and talk to her about what she's done today" or "if you reach a roadblock, ask Lindsey to help you" or simply "if it starts to exceed a couple hours of time, let me know." It's a tough line between managing and specifying resources, but since time is so crucial to your profitability, it is worth specifying how they can use this as a valuable resource.

To be clear, when you use these three suggestions, it doesn't have to be clunky or placed in a form. They are guides for you in the way you communicate with those you work with. So, for example, it may simply be stated in the e-mail:

"Stacia, could you pull together a quick analysis for ABC client? The client wants to know the five largest nonprofits that are also working in the family-service space in Detroit, what services they are offering, and where in the city they offer those services. The information will be used by the board to make a decision about a foundation grant, so please make sure you highlight where there are opportunities to grow in service to families within the city. I'm going to need this by next Wednesday; let me know if that's not going work. Also, you may want to take an hour or so to talk with Samantha about what she's learned today in her work with the client. And take a look at the client's strategic plan on Dropbox."

Always be protective of your client relationships. Remember the Bull's-eye—at its heart are referrals, reups, and upsales. This is where you are going to build your business in the fastest, most economical way possible. This is also totally dependent on your customer relationships. That is, the value that customers believe you can continue to produce for them year after year, and in a consistent, high-quality way. Accordingly, be cautious about any contact with your client, even if it is simply an e-mail. I find that I wait months or even sometimes over a year before I let an associate write a direct client e-mail. It may seem overly controlling, but I want my clients to have the best experience possible, and therefore I asked for the correspondence, reports, and interactions to filter through me until I'm fully confident. Even after I'm confident, I always try to be the last person to look at documents and other key deliverables before they go to a customer. At the end of the day, I know Civitas Strategies lives or dies based on those relationships, and I need to have "the buck stops here" attitude around those things that are going to most influence client relationships, whether in a positive or negative way.

TRAINING BY WATCHING AND LISTENING

Whether they are consultants or employees, training is not an easy undertaking for the small to medium consultancy. This is particularly true when you are a nonprofit consultancy and your profit margins are so tight that you don't have a human resources department or the ability to engage trainers.

I greatly struggled with this for many years and was essentially limited in my ability to delegate and in turn grow Civitas Strategies. I ended up in a vicious cycle where I needed help in order to grow, but I never seemed to have the time to train people. And much of what I did had a particular flavor to it that precluded me from getting "just anyone" to plug into a project.

I had a breakthrough in a conversation with Mark Asofsky, a talented and wise entrepreneur and philanthropist. Mark built an incredible business in an area outside the nonprofit world, and at a young age, he transferred leadership. He was kind enough to spend some time talking to me about that experience and how he did it—and I learned so much.

He had also struggled with the transfer of responsibilities because so much of how he added value involved his hands-on engagement, personal style, and intuition. What eventually worked for him was a variation on the "see one, do one, teach one" approach. I further modified this approach for my work and quickly found that I had a process to help talented people understand the "Civitas Strategies way" and in turn leverage my time in ways that had not been possible before, leading to a 250 percent increase in projects (by dollar value) in one year and subsequent increases year after year.

The way I approach this starts with a particular type of work. For example, I've mentioned that we do many one-on-one qualitative interviews every year. These interviews use an ethnographic approach; they are much more conversational and probing than just running through a series of questions in a survey. When teaching staff how to do interviews, I have them sit in on at least six or seven interviews that I conduct. I am open with the interviewee that this employee is on the call, but ahead of time I ask my colleague not to talk—just to listen and take notes. The notes can be about the content of the conversation, but I ask that the focus be more on what I am asking and how. This is an investment of time and money, but I have found it to be an incredibly valuable one.

We then progress to doing about five interviews where they talk and I remain quiet, unless it is absolutely imperative that I talk. This can be very difficult for me, as I always like these interviews and want to take a lead role in them. But it is crucial for me to listen to how my associates conduct interviews, think about the advice I can give them later about their technique, and most importantly give them the opportunity to spread their wings and gain confidence. It is only after these two steps that they can then start conducting interviews unsupervised. But even during the first two or three months of unsupervised interviewing, I will regularly check in to see how they are doing, not only in terms of project content but in terms of how they are feeling their technique is developing.

EXERCISE EIGHTEEN: TRANSFERRING WISDOM AND CULTURE

Some of you may be lucky enough where the skills that can grow your business the fastest will be ones that are easily found and require little internal training or enculturation. However, most of you will probably have some specific way that you're doing things or approaching things that differentiates you from other firms and adds significant value for your clients. For those of us in the latter category, we need a way to transfer that wisdom and culture, even if the given team member may have existing relevant skills. The method that follows can take weeks or even a couple of months depending on how regularly you apply yourself, but it is well worth the time invested.

- **Step One: Select the Task or Skill to Transfer**—I typically suggest clients start on the tasks that will leverage the greatest amount of their time while also being the easiest to potentially transfer. In other words, those skills that are going to free up the greatest amount of your time while taking the least time to train someone. As you complete one skill with an employee or contractor, you can move to increasingly more difficult ones, and you will find he or she will typically learn faster than anticipated because of the skills already gained.
- **Step Two: Observe Practice**—You're going to need to commit to having that person observe you using that skill for a certain amount of time or a certain number of instances. I found that if somebody is truly ready to take on the given practice, he or she can observe it anywhere from five to ten times and learn it effectively, depending on the complexity. You will also want to debrief with your team member at least half the time, if not after every instance, to understand what is being learned and that he or she is on track. Though this is time consuming, resist the opportunity to move to step three before the number of instances are completed—many times you or your team member want to move too quickly, so keep on the course you set.
- **Step Three: Practice**—Once you've completed step two, you can use a much shorter number of instances, usually fewer than five, to observe your team member using that skill. Though it may be hard, do not intervene unless you truly believe your client relationship or the entire success of a project is at stake. This may mean that you let staff make mistakes, but if they're not

significant, let them happen, and use them as fodder for learning in your debrief. Assuming that they are successful in your set number of observations, let them begin to work independently, but check in with them at least once a month for the first three to four months to see how they are applying the skills and what they're learning.

Again, I'm the first to admit that this is a time-consuming way to bring team members up to speed—and this after I'm always harping on profitability! But this is a great opportunity to learn from my mistakes and realize that the investment is far more significant in the long run with the time your employees will leverage.

Section IV: Get Growing

You've now gone from a concept and an aspiration to an organization—and one that can grow! But growth is not easy. Rarely does it happen on its own. Instead, like growing a garden, you have to tend it—to monitor and actively engage in it.

In this section, I am going to address growth in multiple ways. I'll start by presenting the control panel—aggregate key data (past, present, and future) so you can always know where you're headed and where you've been to stay on track.

Though the control panel will help you, a Mike Tyson quote comes to mind: "Everyone has a plan until they get punched in the face." Accordingly, I'll also talk about how to use emergent strategy to navigate a shifting landscape.

I'll then show you how you can grow your client base through effective relationship management and service innovation. This is more than just listening to clients; this is about deeply understanding what is driving them and codesigning solutions.

Finally, I'll discuss how you can get the support you need to keep growing—as a professional and entrepreneur—as well as the responsibilities you have to others in the field.

12

The Control Panel

In the past few chapters, we've done a lot of planning to record the strategies and the steps you're going to need to take to realize success. At the end of the day, it's just a document, and it only lives in the world of execution with implementation. Most consultants in the nonprofit world (and leaders for that matter) tend to lean to one extreme or another in implementation—either creating a plan and letting it sit without execution or intuitively executing and figuring things out along the way. I recommend a middle path—where you have the plan and you keep it in mind, but you also know that executing it effectively and spending time in executing, refining, and improving it along the way is where you're going to have the greatest success. The best way to do that is to have good data about what you are executing and how you are doing so far—this is where the control panel comes in.

The control panel is the simple format that I've developed over the years to provide the key data you need—past, present, and future—at your fingertips to guide your organization. It is bigger than a dashboard but far shorter and more streamlined than a full strategic plan.

The control panel will have four sections:

- Goals
- Annual objectives
- Project lifecycle and major milestones
- Sales goal and pipeline

The format you use is up to you—it could be a Microsoft Word document, an Excel spreadsheet, or even PowerPoint slides. What is critical is having the data at your fingertips and keeping it updated. And, of course, looking at it and using it as a guide for your decisions and activities.

Let's delve into each component in greater detail.

GOALS

I find that the terms "goals" and "objectives" can be very similar to the word "strategy"—and that the definition and usage can vary greatly. Try not to get hung up on the definition, but rather focus on how goals can drive and guide your work.

I'm not a fan of having a large number of goals. On the other hand, having just one goal can be too limiting, especially for consultancies that focus on both building a business and having social impact. I typically suggest trying to identify three goals:

- **Goal (based on the purpose you set in section one)**—I know you are a for-profit, but when you are serving the nonprofit world, chances are much more likely than not that you are motivated by more than a paycheck. Too often, consultancies to nonprofits talk about wanting to have social impact, or claim they do, but refuse to take on any metric. There's a logic here—they aren't the ones providing the services, just the ones helping the service provider. For me (and my clients), that isn't enough. Yes, you can recognize that you aren't the service provider, but you can also challenge yourself to have some measure of your social impact.

  For us at Civitas Strategies, we have taken on a goal of helping our clients serve one million children and families over the next ten years. Our goal recognizes that we are not providing direct services, but rather helping those who help the families and children. Even though we are indirectly and not directly affecting the goal, we wanted to make sure that we were not off the hook for social impact. It is core to the legacy we want to have as an organization. Ask yourself, in ten years, what do you want the legacy of your work to be in terms of social impact? That is your first goal.
- **Sales and Marketing**—This may seem like an abrupt pivot from talking about your social impact, but they're intimately connected. If you want to

have impact, you're going to need projects that give you the opportunity to have impact. So unless you keep on track with your sales and marketing, you won't reach your first goal. I talked about setting sales goals earlier in the book, but look at your new goal, and make sure that you'll be able to make it based on sales.

- **Operations**—Based on what you want to achieve in terms of social impact and your sales and marketing, what are the key operational supports for growth or capacity that you will need? For example, this could mean growing to three or four employees in five years, or it could mean building the capacity to offer a new service within twenty-four months.

ANNUAL OBJECTIVES

To create your annual objectives, take each goal, and break it up year by year from the current year. Within the current year, break down the annual objective into realistic quarterly objectives. For example, let's say you have a goal to serve twenty organizations in two years. You may want to split that goal in half—ten in year one and ten in year two. Then within year one, you may say that the first half of the year will be slower than the remaining parts of the year. Your objectives then could be to work with two organizations in the first quarter, two in the second quarter, three in the third quarter, and three in the fourth quarter. Again, this is not a science, but rather an art, and more about holding yourself accountable to moving forward more than anything else.

PROJECT LIFECYCLE AND MILESTONES

Over the years, I have found it very helpful to have some sort of visual snapshot of the current client projects that I'm working on as well as a list of the biggest milestones we have to meet. This can help you focus not only on what you have to accomplish but also have a quick sense of when you might need help—like a contractor to support a very busy time. Or when you might want to start a new project because currently things are too busy and will be for the next ninety days.

SALES AND MARKETING

You're going to want to track two sets of data for sales and marketing. First, you want to have your overall annual objective and know how much you have secured toward that goal. For example, if your objective for the year is $500,000 in revenue and you already have signed $200,000 in contracts, those are the two numbers you want to use and show also as a percentage (in this case, you have reached 40 percent of your objective).

Second, you want to include your chart using the Pemberton Method that we developed in chapter 8. If you have a particularly large number of prospects, you may want to limit your chart to the top ten or twenty. The main purpose of this is to ensure that you are moving your prospects in the way that you need to and that you are regularly checking so you know that you're moving your pipeline.

EXERCISE NINETEEN: GOAL SETTING

Though there are a few data points on your control panel, let's focus on the most important—goal setting—since it goes to the core of what you are trying to achieve and will be the North Star for you and your team as you navigate growth. Find a quiet place, and set aside an hour or hour and a half. If you have staff, do this exercise yourself first—it's your company and being clear on your vision first and foremost is very important. You are the one person in the entire venture who must believe in this goal.

- **Step One: Set Your Social-Impact Goal**—Start by setting your planning horizon—how long you are giving yourself to meet your goals. Normally, I suggest to clients that they keep goals within a three-year planning horizon. However, this goal is more of an aspirational one—think about five- or ten-year goals. These can be good, but as I said, they tend to be aspirational. The landscape and context you're working in can change greatly in those five years, so chances are you're going to adjust your goals along the way. Having goals for two months will tend to be a lot more concrete. The planning time should be one that you're most comfortable with.

  Next ask the following:
  - What do you want your legacy to be?
  - If in ten, twenty, thirty, or forty years from now you reflect on this venture and say, "I was so proud of what I accomplished," what would the "what" be?
  - What would you want to accomplish regardless of the type of organization (for-profit or nonprofit, consultancy or service provider)?
  - How can this be measured? As mentioned, this may not be straightforward if you don't directly impact your cause. In that case, come up with the closest measure you can, and develop a method for tracking it.
  - Going back to your planning horizon and considering your measure, what is a numerical goal you can commit to that you believe is achievable but also makes you at least a little anxious?

  Remember, this legacy doesn't have to be the grandest in the universe that outshines everyone else—it has to be what would satisfy you.

- **Step Two: Check Your Sales Goal**—In exercise thirteen, you set a sales goal. But now ask yourself, "Will this goal give me the velocity to reach my social-impact goal?" This may not be simple or straightforward—it will be more of a gut check. If you are unsure, you'll probably want to redo step one and set a goal that is more realistic. You will want to push yourself and your firm on both goals, but you don't want to do this so much that you actually hurt the firm by taking on too big of a social-impact goal. Similarly, you don't want to take on a sales goal that demands so much time that your client services slack off.

- **Step Three: Set Your Operations Goal**—Finally, you need to ask if you have the resources you need to reach your social-impact and sales goals. Consider the planning horizon you set in step one:
  - Will you need additional technology or systems?
  - What kind of talent will be needed?
  - Will you eventually need to take on other major changes to your business model, like adding an office or finding talent based in another region?
  - Off all the resources you identified, which are the ones (one to three) that will be most crucial to meeting your goals?

  Again, you will want to check in on your social-impact and sales goals in light of the resource needs to see if one or the other needs to be adjusted.

- **Step Four: Test with Staff**—As mentioned in the opening of this exercise, this is best conducted initially by you and any other partners or principals. It should also be shared with your team. You can blame sharing it after on me! Let them know you needed to clarify the vision, but it is also important to get their perspectives and reactions. When you review it with them, ask if the goals possess the following characteristics:
  - **Realistic**—Does the team see them as achievable (but at the same time, a stretch)?
  - **Inspiring**—Do they want to wake up every day and be a part of making this happen?
  - **Overwhelming**—Do the goals push the team, or are they so intimidating that they panic?

  Again, adjust all three goals as needed so they can now be annualized.

- **Step Five: Annualize into Objectives**—Take each of your goals, and per-form the following:
  - ○ Make it an annual objective for each year in your planning horizon. So if you had a ten-year planning horizon, you have ten individual years of goals. Don't sweat this too much—the exercise is about getting to your current year goal. It is less important to know the objective in 2026 than it is to know that more of the goal will be met later than sooner or that it is evenly distributed each year.
  - ○ Within the current-year objective, break it into quarterly goals—again, this could vary in distribution. If you are a start-up, you may want to have lower first- and second-quarter goals to accommodate all the activities needed to gain momentum. If you are an established company, you may want to spread the objective evenly or by past experience (e.g., maybe there is a degree of seasonality to your work).

USING YOUR CONTROL PANEL

Your control panel is only as good as your data and how often you use it. Always keep it current, and use it at least on a weekly basis. This will help you know how you and your team should spend your time, how other resources should be used, and how you should react to changes in the environment. Therefore, you can't just pull it out in an emergency—you have to constantly be looking at it and sweating it. I strongly suggest setting a firm time every week to review it (for us at Civitas Strategies, it is every Monday—a motivation for the week ahead).

You also have to remember the control panel is just a guide—it helps you to direct the plane, but ultimately you have to fly it and make decisions that go beyond it or were never even considered when you created it. This is the art of emergent strategy, which I will discuss in the next chapter.

13

Your Frenemy: Emergent Strategy

When most people think about strategy, they think about something static—plans that you create that are somehow going to guide you over five years. But we know that things change, sometimes only days after you finish creating that plan.

But that isn't the full story about strategy. There is deliberate strategy, which is what almost every one of you is familiar with—the strategy that you planned out ahead of time and guides your implementation over time. Fewer people know about emergent strategy—this is the strategy that you craft in reaction to changes in the environment. If your purely using emergent strategy instead of a strategic plan, you usually have tenets or some sort of principles to guide your decisions around strategy. In my practice, I have found that you need a combination of the two—you need the North Star (provided by deliberative strategy) but also the tenets that guide you when the world shifts out from under you.

OPPORTUNITIES AND TANGENTS

I titled this chapter as a warning about emergent strategy—one that shouldn't be underemphasized. Emergent strategy can be incredibly powerful in helping you to take advantage of opportunities that appear and were never anticipated. One example is the original wave of the US Department of Education Investing in Innovation Fund grants released during the Great Recession as part of the economic stimulus plan. The grant was a departure from most past programs in that it demanded that programs be grounded in research, evaluated through rigorous methods, innovative, and nationally scalable. It didn't fit into the box of how many programs saw themselves or their work (i.e., they didn't see their efforts as innovative or how they could become innovative).

The same could be said of consultants advising programs that wanted to apply—even the grant itself required fresh interpretation, since the language and format departed from what was previously used. By using the emergent strategy, as I'll describe, a significant number of organizations saw the opportunity for what it was and invested resources in trying to pursue it. But not all chose to pursue it, because it just didn't fit their preconceived notions of the grants that they wanted to hunt.

But there's also a dark side to emergent strategy. It can easily become a way to justify following opportunities that quickly become a tangent that pulls you away from the course you need to take to sustain and grow your business. This is especially true when you opt to go "all in" on an opportunity and commit an inordinate amount of resources to it.

Another consultant I know had a great firm serving nonprofits that was doing well for years. The firm hit a lull in work, and the team began to panic. The owner and his senior consultants began to search for new opportunities outside of their core markets. Every time there was a hint of a new opportunity, the firm ramped up research of all the potential targets, understood the field, and cold-called potential clients. Before the strategy could fully play out, another new market would be found and again chased, while the previous market was quickly set aside. Each subsequent opportunity was dropped before knowing if it was fertile ground or not, resulting in no new projects and the quick consumption of the firm's sales budget. In turn, this made the situation even more dire and eventually forced a significant reduction in the firm's size.

As you navigate your world using emergent strategy, I want you to keep both examples in mind—both the promise and the peril.

USING EMERGENT STRATEGY

How do you use emergent strategy? There are four variables I recommend considering.

- **Always Listen and Learn**—Explore any opportunity ahead of time by reading what you can and also by talking to people in your network who can test the idea with you. You may quickly learn that the opportunity is not as good as it seems on the surface, or conversely, you may see how great an opportunity it is. Keep in mind the window for an opportunity may be a small one, so your research may not be extensive. But no matter how little time you do have, you should at least try to learn up front (rather than after you are committed).

- **Know Your Core and Your Limits**—Clearly define up front what is core to your consultancy—not only what you do well (your core competencies) but also how you are going to do it (your core values). You also want to define where you will not go. That is, any limitation where you draw a line between your firm and any opportunity that may emerge. For example, there may be a geographical, service, or ethical limit to what you will pursue.
- **Limit Your Exposure and Risk**—Emergent strategy is often about reacting quickly. Though an opportunity may be great, you also don't want to commit all or a significant part of your resources to a strategy that is untested and created quickly. Only commit the resources you can afford to lose, so if the strategy doesn't pay off, you still have your core clients and projects to sustain the organization.
- **Learn and Decide**—Carefully watch your implementation of emergent strategy to learn how it is doing. If it doesn't play out to your benefit, don't hesitate to pull out or refine the strategy. Just because you chose the course at one point in time doesn't mean that you are committed for eternity. If it does clearly benefit your firm, you may want to consider putting more resources, incrementally, into the opportunity. That is, even if things are going well, you still want to be cautious about putting in more resources so you don't put your organization's future at risk.

Remember, emergent strategy is about seeing an opportunity and (if it makes sense) trying it out to see if it is good for your consultancy. It isn't about a pivot and dedicating all or even a majority of your effort to a strategy that is being built as you do it.

EXERCISE TWENTY: NAVIGATING WITH EMERGENT STRATEGY

This exercise can be used whenever an opportunity arises that you may want to pursue. I would suggest doing step one up front, since you'll want to make sure you set parameters ahead of time, not in the heat of the moment. Feel free to record your responses to step one here in the book, so you'll have it nearby.

Allow forty-five to ninety minutes to assess the opportunity. If you are doing it alone, you will want a quiet space. However, this is also an exercise you may want to run with your team. To be clear, I'm not suggesting that if you have a team, you need to include them, but just that you *may* want to do the exercise with them. At the end of the day, it is your firm, so you may want to evaluate a big opportunity alone without any influence one way or another.

- **Step One: Set Limits**—For the first part of this step, write down your services. You have already worked earlier in the book to get them to a concise list, and you've been practicing with them, so this should come from memory. Your services will provide a visual reminder of what is the core of your current business.

  Now let's turn to the limits of where you are willing to go. This step will be similar to your must-haves/must have nots but will be solely focused on your consultancy and the limits of where you are willing to take it. Write down all the answers you can come up with to the question, "What are the types of projects that I do not want to pursue, no matter what?" Specifically consider the following:
  - geographic limits (e.g., maybe you are a regional firm because you don't want to fly)
  - project scope (e.g., as mentioned previously, I limited Civitas Strategies from talent search for years)
  - project size (i.e., there may be some projects that financially are too small to be viable)
  - ethical limits (e.g., the Association of Fundraising Professionals requires you to reject fund-raising projects where you are paid a percentage of the gift you secure)
  - any other factor you want to include

Now look at the list, and begin to consolidate your answers or eliminate minor ones. Your goal is to get the list down to around three to five items that will guide you—keep cutting until you get there, even if it means making difficult choices. You want to set limits, but you don't want to create blinders to opportunities that could arise.

- **Step Two: Define the Opportunity**—Find out what you can about the opportunity at hand. This could be very limited, since you don't have much time. If the opportunity isn't pressing, research it on the Internet, and talk to people in your network. Do your best to understand the good and the bad it presents.

  Record the results of your research by answering the following questions:

  - **How much time and resources will it take to pursue the opportunity?** It may be that you will have to answer within twenty-four hours. On the other side of the spectrum, you may have to respond to a lengthy request for proposals and then face a nine-month review process. Be very specific in your answers so you know exactly what will be at risk.

  - **What is the probability of getting the outcome you want?** You're considering the opportunity because it is possible, but how probable is it? Do you have a very significant chance or one in one hundred? Write it as a percentage, and when in doubt, estimate lower rather than higher.

  - **What is the long-term potential of the opportunity?** If you are successful in pursuing the opportunity and start gaining momentum, what is the possible benefit over the next two years? Are you opening a whole new market, or is it only an opportunity that will exist for a short time?

- **Step Three: Assess and Decide**—Now you have to make a decision on moving forward. I can't make that decision for you, but I can point to some questions to consider based on the results from steps one and two:

  - Is the opportunity "out of bounds" and beyond the limits you set?

  - Does it align in some way with your core services? As we learned from the Bull's-eye, you want to be able to sell it to existing customers. Can this opportunity engage any of your existing market or vice versa? Does it open up a new market that would buy at least some of your existing services?

- ○ Are you willing to potentially lose all the resources needed to pursue the opportunity and potentially get nothing in return if it doesn't work out? Will your firm still be healthy?
- ○ What is the cost of the opportunity? What won't you get done while you are pursuing the opportunity?

- **Step Four: Set Up the Test**—If you complete step three for any opportunities that you want to pursue, next set up the parameters of your test before moving forward. Recall what I said earlier—emergent strategy is about going into unknown territory, so you do it by testing first before you jump in whole hog. Set the parameters of your test around the following dimensions:
  - ○ What is the upper limit of the money you're willing to invest?
  - ○ What is the greatest amount of time you are going to invest in pursuing the opportunity?
  - ○ What result will be attractive enough for you to continue pursuing the opportunity? Do you need a certain level of profit or size of a contract to enable you to say this is worth trying again?

Write down the answers to the questions, and set a time, even if it is a year or more out, to revisit and assess your test against the parameters you set.

EMERGENT STRATEGY IN PRACTICE

Navigating emergent strategy can be difficult, so let me provide an example of how it played out for a past Civitas Strategies client. I've changed some of the broad strokes of the story to preserve confidentiality.

Back in 2013, a client considered getting into the business of Head Start community assessments. Head Start grantees are required to conduct a community assessment every three years as part of the application process. Starting in 2013 (and continuing for years after), the US Department of Health and Human services, which manages the Head Start program, forced the largest competition of the largest number of Head Start grantees since the program's inception. Our client had heard from a peer in another part of the United States that this recompletion was driving demand for consulting to help perform community assessments that far outstripped the suppliers in the market.

We worked with our client to learn more about the opportunity by researching the regulations and best practices and by talking with other consultants in the field as well as leaders in Head Start agencies. Through our research, we learned that the community assessment did tie to our client's core services—the client provided similar assessments for foundations. We also learned that the time it took to develop the assessments required an initial up-front cost and included recording your methodology, but over time the profit margin increased with replication. The amount that Head Start grantees were going to pay for a community assessment would also more than cover our client's costs, and in fact it would allow the client to offer a product at a lower rate and still make a healthy profit. We also knew that, because of the US Department of Health and Human Services's commitment to recompete so many Head Start grantees, the market would continue for years. Additionally, when the recompetes were over, grantees were still required to do it every three years, providing the potential for sustained work.

We then discussed what the client was going to put at risk to pursue this opportunity. One of the things that we heard clearly from our research gathering was that Head Start grantees only wanted to engage consultants who had previously performed community assessments. As a result, our client decided to test the opportunity by putting the resource of time at risk. The client tried to sell its community assessment product for five hours a month for six months. If no contract was secured by then, our client would let the opportunity go. Our client wanted to put more hours into the opportunity, but this was the upper limit where it wouldn't interfere with selling core products and services and risk the entire enterprise.

At the end of six months, there were no takers. The fact that our client was new to the product created too much of a risk for Head Start grantees. Though our client wasn't able to realize the opportunity, there were no regrets because it put to rest any questions about the market potential. At the same time, no long-term harm came to the firm.

Don't hesitate to use the "power of no." I want you to grow your business, and that means pursuing new opportunities. But I also want you to sustain your business, and sometimes the best way to do that is by saying no.

14

Growth through Relationships

I've previously talked about sales and marketing as being the immediate activities for sustaining and growing your consultancy. There's a third way to generate growth opportunities that has emerged: business development. The discipline of business development is still in the early stages compared with the venerable fields of sales and marketing. Business development is gaining momentum in the private sector because it is working to support growth.

What is business development? There are a number of definitions, but most simply it is the pursuit of relationships and partnerships to create growth opportunities within and between organizations.

For most consultancies serving nonprofits, which are typically lean on staff, there are two ways to pursue the principles of business development: through relationships with complementary service providers and through your current and past customers. I also want to expand your thinking about client relationships to include growth through service innovation—creating new solutions to your customer's challenges.

THE POWER OF PARTNERSHIPS

At the center of the Bull's-eye were those who knew your value the most, and the next circle contained referrals that you got where a trusted, shared contact vouched for you. These types of connections can happen through your customers as you build your base. But you can also accelerate the number of referrals you get through partnerships with complementary organizations and consultants.

There are three assumptions at play here. First, that you don't do everything— there are going to be other firms that, whether they're in your field or not, serve the same niche but in a different way, where you're not competing. The second assumption is that, just like you, these firms are looking for referral opportunities. The third assumption is that your customers will value a referral by you to another organization just as much as that other organization's customers will value their referral to you.

Many times when I talk to consultants in the nonprofit world about these types of relationships they are blasé about it. Typically, they will say that they do know other consultants and that these other consultants know them, so the referrals can already happen.

However, the most active partners I have for referrals are those where the reciprocity has been actively cultivated over time. That's a nice way of saying that I make it a point to refer to organizations that I've selected as partners. This activity helps to move our relationship to a new level, where they see the benefit of referrals and are much more likely to make them.

Additionally, typical consultant networks develop incrementally. They remain fairly static. When they do add new partners, it's usually ad hoc—maybe they meet at a conference or are on the same team in a larger project. I recommend that you hunt for partners just as you would customers. This is an opportunity for you to not only build your base of referrals and your network but also once more add value to your clients. Since you should be hunting for those providers who provide services that are most difficult for your clients to find, when you refer them, you are simultaneously helping both the partner organization and your client build the relationship into the future.

Let me give you a quick example from my firm, Civitas Strategies. We serve a lot of organizations in the education world, and if there's one trend in funding that I would lift up above all others over the past ten years, it is the push for evidence. Whether it's a government grant or private foundation, funders want to see evaluation data up front, and they want grantees to include rigorous evaluations in their projects. However, evaluations can be expensive, and not all evaluators are easy to work with. My firm does some evaluations, specifically implementation evaluations, but not the outcome evaluations, which are in great demand. Accordingly, I make it a point to seize any opportunity I have to meet and vet new outcome-evaluation consultants. Numerous times I've been able to refer them to my clients, making a positive connection for all involved. As you may imagine from this description, the strategy is not particularly time consuming, but it certainly does pay off.

Let me be clear—when you make a referral, you are vouching for that other organization and vice versa. When you refer other firms to one of your clients, you're staking your brand and reputation—the most valuable things your firm has. If it's a partner you know well and potentially even used, this may be relatively easy. But if this is a new partnership, you may want to approach it similar to emergent strategy, where you're cautious about how many referrals you make and you wait to receive feedback on customer experience before moving further.

BUILDING YOUR CUSTOMER RELATIONSHIPS—CHECKING IN

Maintaining relationships, especially when you include both your current and your former customers, can be someone's full-time job. However, this is a luxury few of you will be able to afford. Knowing how tight your time is, I recommend one strategy that you can undertake to maximize the time that you do have—the customer check-in.

It may seem obvious, but you can't listen to your clients and build relationships with them if you aren't talking to them. Accordingly, you need to make sure that there is time to listen to customers—before, during, and after an engagement. This really is a discipline. It is so easy as you move from project to project to focus on getting the work done and not taking the time to listen, especially since it may not seem like the greatest use of your time when you're going full-bore to keep up on everything you're trying to accomplish. But you need to do it. It is difficult to be disciplined about it, but conversations and listening are going to be your number-one way to keep in the Bull's-eye and ensure that your sales and marketing pipeline is always moving forward.

CUSTOMER CONVERSATIONS

I recommend two different ways of engaging your clients to deepen the relationship: regular check-ins with current customers and periodic conversations with former customers.

For current clients, I suggest having at least weekly check-ins by e-mail, by telephone, or in person. This contact can be very short—for example, an e-mail letting them know that you are still in the process of putting their final report together and are on track for the meeting in two weeks. If you call or meet, have some talking points or an agenda at hand. The primary benefit is that the contact reminds the customer that you are important to them. Secondarily, it can give you important intelligence on your current project and potential new ones. I never cease to be amazed at how many times my e-mail or call will prompt a response about an issue or concern that may have festered had the client not had the opportunity to communicate. I also learn about new problems that I can solve for them. Clients will often see you in the same way you see your room looking through a keyhole—in a very narrow point of view. On some level, they may be aware that you do other things, but they tend to affiliate you with those services and products from which they have derived direct value.

For example, I know a consultancy that provides an array of communications services. It was engaged by a client to develop a website, and the consultancy became known as the "web people." The client didn't really see beyond the website-development service. By asking about how the client was doing, the owner found out about a need for a larger communications plan and was able to pitch her firm to do it. As a trusted source, her client was excited by the idea and engaged her consultancy for the additional work.

Once your project is completed, you should continue to periodically and systematically reconnect with your former customer. This contact can be by e-mail, by telephone, or in person. But no matter how it is done, it should be based around value for your customer—not for you. This could be small, like an article or a piece of news you heard about a former colleague, or large, such as an emerging trend you have found or a connection you want to personally facilitate with a potential funder. Regardless, ensure that you have set time frames for circling back on a regular basis.

To be clear, the benefits are twofold. For your former clients, they're getting value—large and small, free of charge, and when they may least expect it. In return, for you, you're giving them subtle reminders of the positive experience they had and that you're still out there. That last point cannot be underrated—most referrals happen while you're top of mind. That means it's most likely to happen soon after your project (while your customer's experience is still recent and fresh) or when there is some reason to think of you again—these contacts provide that reason.

Just as you are systematically checking in with your clients, you also may want to find ways to systematically generate the value you can offer them. Again, this doesn't have to be very difficult. One way to do it is to set up a Google news alert on a subject that is important to them and be able to share that pertinent information. At Civitas Strategies, every time we get a new client we set up a Google news alert on that organization and topics that are related. Many times the alerts are not worthwhile, but occasionally we see ones that are, especially when they mention the organization. You'd be surprised how many of our clients don't even know that they've come up in the news.

Another example is the daily grant surveillance that we perform for every client and former client of Civitas Strategies. Everyone in the nonprofit world is always looking for new opportunities for funding. For us, it is a relatively easy process. It is one of the best investments of time that we make—one e-mail a day from the federal government and one e-mail a day from a proprietary-grants database for which we pay only a few hundred dollars a year. But for our customers, it is a huge value because they may not know where to look and certainly lack the time and discipline to check every day. Accordingly, they can rest easy knowing we are looking out for their interests and that we have the opportunity to continually and easily generate client value and help, albeit in a small way, to extending their impact.

EXERCISE TWENTY-ONE: CREATING YOUR RELATIONSHIP SYSTEM

The relationships you have, maintain, and strengthen are going to be instrumental to the growth of your organization. Accordingly, I recommend setting up your own system of policies and procedures to regularly build your relationships. This exercise will take about an hour to complete. It can be done just by you or together with your team.

- **Step One: Set a Check-In Policy**—Determine how often you're going to check in with current clients. I recommend weekly, but this may not work for your firm. Whatever time you set, make it a habit to set a reminder in your to-do system to help you execute it as you intend. If you don't already have a firm system in place, stop right now, and contact each one of your clients. Again, this could be a simple e-mail saying, "we're making progress and wanted to make sure you knew." There's no need to spend hours doing it, but if you haven't done it in a while, do it right now.

- **Step Two: Systematically Reconnect with Former Clients**—If you're just starting up, write a policy on how you want to do this—this could just be a few bullets in a note to yourself and a reminder to start engaging former clients. Your timeline can be three, six, nine, or twelve months from now—whatever makes sense for your firm and when you will start having former clients. For existing consultants, I recommend dividing your former clients into three categories and setting a frequency for how often you are going to connect with them:

  - **The Inner Circle**—It includes clients who are your strongest advocates and referral sources. I have found that most consultancies get a disproportionate number of referrals from just a few sources. Inner-circle members may be people you want to contact every one or two months.

  - **Fans**—They consist of former clients who are very positive about you but may not have provided a referral. Or they may not be in the position to refer you at this moment. For fans, you may want to contact them once a quarter or twice a year.

  - **The Outer Circle**—Maybe there are some customers who were satisfied but not over-the-top happy or who have moved into positions that are outside your field. In these cases, reach out to them at least once a year.

  For each category, set up assignments on your to-do system. Designate who will pursue each task, and make sure that the task recurs for the appropriate period. For example, you may have "time to reach out to Jeanne Smith," which when completed will recur every three months. This will streamline the amount of time it takes to maintain the system.

- **Step Three: Find Complementary Organizations**—Start by listing all the firms with which you already have a relationship. Think about any way that you can make a referral for at least one quarter of your list in the next month.

    Then, list the types of firms that your clients have trouble connecting with (e.g., grant writers or graphic artists are common needs). Select the one or two types that are most frequent. Reach out to your professional network for connections to firms that could potentially fill those gaps in the future. You could do this actively by e-mailing some people who you think will have ideas or even by putting up a post on LinkedIn or Facebook asking for suggestions. Make the time to have a call with the most promising of the firms sent to you. There will probably be a large number, so limit each call to thirty minutes.

During the call, follow these steps:

- o Be open about why you were seeking to connect with them—for future potential referrals for your clients.
- o Ask them to describe their services. You may have already reviewed their website or other documents, but I always find it particularly helpful to hear consultants describe their own mix of services in order to get a sense of where they think their strengths are greatest.
- o Ask them which clients they are most successful with—you don't want to set up a situation where they're going to be great for the referral, take it, and then not succeed because it's an unusual or uncomfortable situation for them.
- o If you feel confident in the contact, end the call by committing to refer each other in the future and also setting a time to reconnect and catch up. This doesn't have to be in the near term; it could be six months out. But it will give you a chance to reconnect and remain top of mind.

I was recently talking with a consultant in the technology sector about using this exercise for his firm. The information was incredibly helpful to him, and he noted the transferability to any for-profit consultancy (i.e., outside the non-profit world). I second that thought and also add that the same system can be used with your nonprofit clients for their resource-development efforts.

SERVICE INNOVATION

With all the contact you have with your clients and former clients, you are going to hear feedback on services and products—yours, competitors', and ones your clients wished were out there. This intelligence provides a crucial opportunity for growth. Remember back in chapter 1 when I suggested you limit your services and products? Now is the time to start changing that and carefully add to your offerings.

I am honing in on service innovation in this section on purpose. To be clear, I define service innovation as changing, adapting, or evolving an existing product or service so that it is more effective or efficient. It is fundamentally different from invention, which is creating something entirely new, or replication, which is adding service and doing it in the same way as other firms. Invention and replication have their place, but for consultancies like ours, service innovation can take less effort and fewer resources than it would take to invent something entirely new, but it is also more differentiated than merely replicating.

As crude as it may sound, your service innovation goal should be to do that service "faster, better, or cheaper" than others in the market. This can be achieved by internal (i.e., the client doesn't see it) or external (the client experiences changes) means. Internally, you could create new processes that allow you to use lower-level staff or integrate technology, both of which could drive down costs. Looking at the external experience, you might offer a new way of presenting data so that your clients can use it more effectively, or you might bundle multiple services together to provide a synergy among them.

Keep in mind that whatever you do should be faster, better, or cheaper, but it may not be all three. That is, you can have a service that is more effective and faster but then demands a higher price.

There are many great books out there on how to develop services or products. At the very least, you should be familiar with *Lean Startup* by Eric Ries, *Business Model Generation* by Alexander Osterwalder and Yves Pigneur, and *Will It Fly?* by Pat Flynn. I won't repeat the great knowledge you can mine from these works, nor will I try to fit my own here—I could never do it justice in one part of a chapter. But what I will do is outline what the process should look like to help you understand what you need to do in broad strokes.

There are two key tenets I want you to keep in mind throughout. First, that your innovation occurs in reaction to what your customers want and need. This is not about you playing Steve Jobs and declaring that "people don't know what they want until you show it to them." Instead, this is about knowing what is keeping your customers up at night and providing innovations that are attune to their "pains and gains" (i.e., solving a problem or generating greater value).

Second, service innovation should be iterative—similar to the lean-thinking movement from chapter 2, where you developed your MVC. I wouldn't go as far as Reid Hoffman in saying that, "If you are not embarrassed by the first version of your product, you've launched too late." But I do suggest that your innovation shouldn't be perfect when launched. Instead, think of it as an experiment that you implement, learn from, and refine ahead of the next one.

THE PROCESS
Your service innovation should roughly follow a three-step process:

- **Research**—You seek an understanding of the potential "pains and gains"— what is killing your clients in their work and what will have the greatest value if solved. In your conversations with past and former clients, you can reveal this by asking what is keeping them up at night or what they would ideally want out of that service or product (i.e., not just what is out there).
- **Business Model**—With the information you have gained, you can map a business model for your service or product—creating a paper representation or graphic of how it is going to work. I strongly recommend the business model canvass (you can find it by visiting smallbutmighty.com) or using an online version like Strategyzer. This is not as time intensive as it seems and helps ensure you are seeing all the pieces of the business model.

  As you then finalize the business model, circle back to some current or former clients to ask, "Does this work?" Many consultants are reticent about asking their customers' or potential customers' opinions when they are in development. I have found the opposite—if you treat them like a codesigner, they're not only willing to talk to you, they are often excited about being your

very first customers because they know that this solution will be valuable—
they helped build it!

- **Launch and Refine**—Once you have received initial feedback and revised
your business model, it's time to launch and test. Just as I did with emergent
strategy, I recommend doing a limited launch at first. At Civitas Strategies,
when we have a new approach, we only initially use it with existing or former
customers. Since we know them well, this gives us better insights into the
efficacy and how it can be improved. As you get feedback, return to the business model and keep refining it—the result will be a stronger offering with
even greater demand.

An example of how this can play out is in the way that we added talent search to
our services at Civitas Strategies. As I mentioned previously, I originally resisted this. I
believed it was a very challenging area requiring a tremendous amount of specialization. Over the years, clients pushed us to offer talent search. At the same time, the
nonprofit sector was having increasingly greater demand for talent. The field, and the
organizations that needed to operate in it, had gotten more complex. The narrow
profit margin made it difficult to attract talent for compensation alone. Also, at the
most basic level, there were more nonprofit organizations than ever—so even more
demand for talent.

In 2014, a long-time client gave us an ultimatum—the firm needed to hire a
number of mid- and senior-level positions and only trusted Civitas Strategies to do it.
Despite my multiple protests, this client said, "You can do it. You know us, and you're
the only organization we're going to trust to get it done." Who doesn't want to hear
that?

Suddenly, we were in the search business. With one successful project under our
belt, and knowing how many of our clients needed new options for search, I challenged our team to develop a search model that would be as effective, if not better, than existing firms—for half the cost and in half the time. The latter two points
came from customer feedback, which expressed how difficult it was to afford current fees and how lengthy the processes were, even when they could afford a firm.
Using Strategyzer, we created a focused approach, the lean search, which I described
in chapter 10. We tested the model with our customers who had great suggestions

for improving it and also got excited about using lean search. After multiple projects, we found that we were able to provide open-array talent search (per customers' feedback) and then specialized search. And we were able to do it for half the cost and, even better than we hoped, in only 40 percent of the time. This service, built in partnership with our customers, is now one of our best sellers.

15

Developing Your #1 Employee—You

Early in my college career, I was an Army ROTC cadet. Though my time was relatively brief, I learned a lot about leadership that stayed with me throughout my life. Particularly, the maxim that your "soldiers always eat first." Knowing a large number of consultants in the nonprofit world, I've seen that they often live by this motto, always thinking of their team ahead of themselves. At the same time, most of you are going to have consultancies that are based entirely, or at least in very large part, around you.

Your development as a professional and entrepreneur are critical to the growth and survival of your firm. That is why I strongly recommend that you commit to activities that are going to develop you and give you the support you need to survive and thrive.

In counseling my clients, or any professional in the nonprofit sector, I know that the time and money for professional development are limited. To maximize your time, I suggest that each year you undertake two strategies for development—assessing your needs and advancing your capacity through learning and tapping into peer mentoring.

Let's explore each of these in detail.

ASSESSING AND ADVANCING

It's never easy to talk about one's deficits. To assess where you may need to grow, you want to be introspective. But it is also crucial to have outside data. This is not an easy conversation or one you should have with all of your clients. But it may be one that you can have with those you've had a long relationship. You can also turn to your peers (we'll talk more about developing your mentors later in this chapter), since they can provide a safe, external perspective on you.

Finally, you can also gather data that isn't directly from you. One of the services that we offer at Civitas Strategies is assessing development based on professional analogies. That is, looking at the professionals you want to emulate and seeing what they have that you don't. This is as simple as identifying who they are and looking at them on LinkedIn and the Internet to see what characteristics appear to have been important in their success and then aligning them with your existing strengths.

When you've collected all the data, you'll have a list of things you could do to improve yourself. However, there are probably going to be more things that you want to improve than you'll have time to do. Go through your list, and order it by the positive impact each item can have on growing your business. In other words, prioritize what is most likely to save you money or increase your revenue. This is not as obvious as it may seem on the surface, since in some cases it may be about longer-term development goals. For example, you may need to eventually get an advanced degree to gain new clients' respect and business. Focus on the top one or two items on your list. It may be tempting to go further, but leave them for now. If you can check off those first two very quickly, then return to your list. But my guess is between doing client work, having a life, and building your business you will have more than enough to do.

Based on the items you selected, identify ways that you can build your capacity. This could be by learning a new skill or gaining knowledge. In this case, start by looking at all the opportunities you have to learn that skill or gain the knowledge you need. Consider all the significant ways that you can develop yourself, both formal and informal. Try to find what will provide the knowledge in the most direct way possible and, if appropriate, what degree, certification, or certificate can be touted as showing you have that knowledge.

However, your gap may be something different (e.g., being on a board or publishing an article or book). In these cases, start by understanding where you want to go, and find information on the fastest pathway there. Unlike learning, some gaps may be out of your control, but that doesn't preempt you from trying. I had a client who found a gap in a board appointment—other peers were serving on nonprofit boards of directors, and she was not. She couldn't just walk up to a board and say, "I'm on!" She identified some organizations who she knew needed members, networked to current board members she knew, and made it clear that she was interested. Ironically, in the end she didn't get on either of the boards she targeted, but another colleague, knowing she was looking, asked her to be on that board—mission accomplished!

YOU AS BUSINESS OWNER

You're taking a lot of time for your development over the next year, but I want to add one more task—building your business acumen and connections. As I stated in the introduction, almost all consultants in the nonprofit world think of themselves as subject-matter experts and not entrepreneurs. As a result, when they think about development, they typically focus on building their skills and reputations in the field, but not as business owners. I challenge you to do the latter—build your business skills and connections. I'm not suggesting that you have to pursue an MBA or even to go to a business owners' boot camp of some kind. I am suggesting committing to something—just one thing to build your skills and connections. This could include anything from joining your local chamber of commerce to taking an online course.

A LITTLE HELP FROM YOUR FRIENDS

When you look at the majority of business- and professional-development books, they recommend that you have a mentor. It is great advice, but it is much harder to implement. I know few consultants in the nonprofit world with formal, regular mentors. First, they can often be difficult to find. In many cases, that mentor may be accomplished in your field but not knowledgeable about running a business, which is probably where you need the most support (e.g., a professor who is a leader in the early-learning field but has only been in the academy). Second, on the other extreme, are "business" mentors, such as those you find through the US Small Business Administration or chamber-of-commerce programs. Most of the time, these mentors are retirees with experience in growing businesses but ones in other fields. They have limited knowledge of the particulars of the nonprofit world.

We know that having senior mentors to guide you and help you is important, but if they are so hard to find, what do you do? You become the mentor/mentee. You create mentor structures with peers—sometimes being a mentor and guiding them but also having humility and recognizing the need to, at other times, be the mentee and accept advice and critique. Peers may not be as experienced, on the whole, as the traditional mentor, but I have found consultants in the nonprofit arena tend to be like a group of superheroes—where certain ones have strengths that complement others' weaknesses.

THE MENTOR/MENTEE

Being a mentor/mentee is not about having one-off conversations with other professionals. Those may be helpful, but what you really need to grow is sustained engagement. This means committing to an ongoing relationship with another professional in your network to help each other on a regular basis and also as needed when things arise. So how do you find someone to be a fellow mentor/mentee? Look to your professional network. If you weren't using it already, I strongly recommend using LinkedIn. There are many ways to use the system that I won't cover here, but what I will say is that it is a great way to catalog people you know. For those of us from a different generation, it is your Rolodex. Look through LinkedIn, and identify who you trust and who has a similar firm. The best situation will be one in which you have similar challenges but different skills and strengths to offer each other. When you approach potential mentors/mentees, be honest about what you're looking for—chances are they are looking for the same and will be willing commit to mutual support. If they aren't able or interested in doing so, that's all right. At least you know up front that you have to keep searching. If they are interested, test them out for a few months. Set up a time when you can each exchange challenges that you're facing. When you have a few calls under your belt, it will be much easier to start adding in as-needed contact when sudden challenges come up, since now you will know your mentor/mentee and how to best communicate with each other.

YOUR COUNCIL OF SUPERHEROES

The next step in creating your mentor/mentee support system is to create a council of superheroes. A council of superheroes is a group of other similar consultants, again in some way complementary to one another and who, like superheroes, have different strengths that can help the group be stronger than any one of the parts. The advantage of the council of superheroes is that you can tap into multiple minds at once, and you also do it through the commitment to a formal process to accelerate learning. I've run a council of superheroes a number of times over the years and suggest you limit yours to three or four consultants in complementary areas. Think about not only complementary businesses but also geographies (e.g., if you're on the East Coast, try to get somebody on the West Coast) and different places in their business development (so you may have a solo practitioner as well as somebody with a medium-size consultancy). In recruiting the council, start with one peer you know very well, and each commit to finding one other consultant. This will help to broaden your network and also expand the knowledge that you can tap into, and vice versa for your colleague. As much as I would love to say that the council of superheroes should connect every week or every month, I have found that with consultants in the nonprofit world, there are so many demands on your time that it is difficult to commit forever. I have found that after a few weeks, despite the best of intentions, conflicts begin to rise, and before you know it, the council is defunct. Instead, I recommend having everyone commit to a set period. If you have four people, commit to five weekly meetings that are all set ahead of time. This will encourage participation, since everyone will know up front that it is for a limited duration and when it will end. In the first meeting, spend fifteen minutes each talking about where your business is and your greatest challenge. At each subsequent meeting, focus on only one member of the council. She will have the first thirty minutes of the hour to present a challenge or question. In the next twenty-five minutes, the council will provide advice. In the last five minutes, you return to the superhero of the week so she can make commitments to change or action based on the feedback.

Always have one superhero designated to keep track of time and enforce it. If not, the meeting will run way too long, or worse yet get cut off before the superhero of the week can get advice. If the group wants to meet again, I suggest taking at least a month off, if not two. This will help prevent meeting fatigue and the eventual implosion of the council.

EXERCISE TWENTY-TWO: COMMITTING TO YOUR DEVELOPMENT

Your professional development is important, and you should take the time to craft a plan worthy of your business—since your advancement is crucial to sustaining and growing your firm. Set aside an hour to start the plan in a quiet place where you cannot be distracted. This exercise will require some interaction with others, which won't take a lot of time, but you'll want to do it ahead of your planning.

- **Step One: Gather Data**—Start the process by identifying and interviewing at least five clients or peers in your field who you feel you know well enough to engage in a conversation about your development. Ask them the following:
  - ○ Where do I have the greatest opportunity for professional growth?
  - ○ When you look at other consultants in similar fields, do they have knowledge, capacity, or skills I lack?
  - ○ If you get out your crystal ball and look into the future, what is the one skill you think consultants like myself will need to have more than any other?

  Next, select three professionals who you would want to emulate. I suggest picking someone who is about ten years your senior. Pull information on them from LinkedIn and their biography. If you have contacts in common, take the time to ask them why they think that person is so successful in terms of their skills or abilities. As you review the information you've collected, try to find no more than five characteristics that you see as being instrumental in that person's success. Consider all the factors, such as their
  - ○ education level;
  - ○ authorship (not only if they have publications, but which types and which have the greatest "buzz");
  - ○ contributions to the field;
  - ○ speaking engagements and webinars;
  - ○ volunteer and philanthropic activities; and
  - ○ professional-association participation.

  Take the five characteristics you identified, and compare them with your background. Add them to the list you collected in your conversations with peers and clients. Prioritize the list based on each professional-development opportunity's potential impact on growing your business, either by reducing costs or by increasing revenues. Pick the top one or two items for development throughout the year.

- **Step Two: Find Advancement Opportunities**—Focusing on the top two priorities for development, identify one learning opportunity that you can pursue that will best fill the gap, and, if possible, show others that you have the skill (such as a certification). Consider both formal and informal ways to achieve your goals, such as the following:

  - **Join an Association**—Many associations include opportunities to build your capacity through online and in-person courses, events, or peer learning, to serve on boards and committees and be published in their journals.

  - **Pursue a Degree or Certification**—In some cases you may need to go back to school. If that is the case, try to get some sort of credential or certificate that you can promote as showing you have that skill.

  - **Share Knowledge**—I increasingly hear from the nonprofit field that there is a need to show that you are building knowledge in the field. This could mean publishing a book or journal article, but it could also mean a blog entry (as a guest or your own) or having a framework or diagram that you can tout. (Don't underestimate this last point. Many times the thought leaders in your field won't have a book but instead a figure that shows something others have missed.)

  - **Online Courses**—I am a secret (or not so secret now) course addict. I always enjoy learning, and I have found that I can find courses on almost any subject, taught by leaders in the field, and that I can learn at any time. For example, when our second son was born, I took classes while doing late-night feedings—I did so many that I earned a multicourse certificate.

  When in doubt, ask others how they filled that gap, or search online for ways to do it. Chances are someone has a pathway to get there.

- **Step Three: Commit to Improving Your Business Acumen and Network**—Choose at least one thing you will do to develop yourself as a business owner. Let me give you two suggestions that are relatively easy—if nothing else, pick one of these:

○ **Join an Association**—There are many business-owner associations that can provide you with valuable information, benefits, and networking opportunities. If you work where you live, consider joining your local chamber of commerce. Many of the other members will be in retail, banking, or other sectors of the economy, but you can still learn from them, and their connections can be valuable to you personally and professionally. Another association to consider is the Freelancers Union. You may not define yourself as a freelancer, but think of it more as an association for microbusinesses like yours. The focus is on the service industry and firms where you are the main, if not the only, resource. So, almost everything the Freelancers Union produces can be informative.

○ **Gain Specific Knowledge**—This could be as simple as reading a book or taking a course. If you're not sure what to read, take a look at our website—I've provided some suggestions and reviews (www.smallbut-mightybook.com). The more you know about your business, the better off you will be.

• **Step Four: Identify Mentor/Mentees**—Look through your LinkedIn contacts, or whatever system you use, to see who you know. You may feel that you know everyone who is a potential mentor/mentee, but many times you may forget people who would be wonderful candidates—take the time to go through your contacts. Look for those people who

○ you respect;

○ have a similar, but not competing, consultancy—even better, if it has a complementary service where you can cross-refer;

○ you believe have skills and knowledge that you lack and vice versa; and

○ you enjoy talking to—this is a person with whom you may spend a fair amount of time on the phone or having coffee, so make sure that this is somebody whose company you enjoy.

Reach out to the person for a meeting or call. On the call, lay out what you're looking to do—create a reciprocal relationship where you can help each other's businesses grow by supporting and developing each other. Commit to at least one call every other month for six months. On these calls, be prepared to share a particular concern or question, and ensure that there's ample time for both of you to put something out on the table.

- **Step Five: Create a Council of Superheroes**—Starting with one peer, agree to recruit two other consultants to the council. Make sure up front that you're looking for people who will be complementary to you in their services, geography, or some other variable; they should be people who are not competitors and who will provide referral opportunities. Commit to a series of five, one-hour telephone calls or meetings, and set them all up ahead of time. Use the protocol I described previously to give each person a chance to gain counsel. Convene at least one council of superheroes a year. If you want to do more than one, select new members, if possible, to add to your network and gain new insights.

PAY IT FORWARD

I started this chapter by talking about how difficult it is to find a mentor in the nonprofit consulting world. I challenge all of you reading this book to change that dynamic and commit to mentor someone more junior than you in the field. The only way to change the culture is by being part of that change. This does not mean that you have to engage in the weekly mentorship of somebody for six years, but this does mean that when others need your help in the nonprofit field, you help them. Share your knowledge, share your skills, and help others to realize the kind of service that they want for themselves and their organization. Remember, there's a lot that you have to offer, not only your knowledge of the field and network but even things that transcend sectors—such as how to job hunt, write an effective résumé, or network. These are all things that can benefit your junior colleagues, so please share your wisdom.

Conclusion

I love my job.

I enjoy making a living by helping people, learning new things, and being able to do it all while still being an actively engaged father and husband. Don't get me wrong, not every day is kittens and rainbows, but the sunny days far exceed the cloudy ones. This is why I wanted to write this book—so you can find the same enjoyment out of consulting as I do, and so that you can do it sustainably for as long as you want.

If nothing else, I hope you've learned the following:

1. **You can create and grow a profitable public-service consultancy that will have social impact**—No one in the stories I've shared, including myself, is all that different from you. We have different strengths and weaknesses, and we developed them into a business model and firm. If we can do it, you can too!

2. **As you build your consultancy, you can integrate your life and work together without sacrificing one to the other**—I started this book talking about the criticality of lifestyle integration, and it is fitting to include it in the conclusion. Just as your public-service consultancy should have public impact, it should also have personal impact—supporting the life you want for yourself and your family. This will not always be easy. There are times you will need to learn how to say no, to your clients and yourself, but in the end it will be well worth it.

3. **None of this happens if you don't take action**—Think of yourself as a shark: if you don't keep moving, you will die. No matter what, even if it is just an hour a week, develop your plan and keep executing. When I first started Civitas Strategies, I only dedicated four hours a week to it. The time added up, and before I knew it, I had a full-time endeavor. It happens one step at a time.

So get moving! And know that you are not alone. I'm always up for an e-mail or conversation about your consultancy. Honestly, I love the business and probably will enjoy the call even more than you will! To find a time to connect, e-mail me at gary@smallbutmightybook.com.

Also, join the community online at smallbutmightybook.com. On the site, you'll be able to find additional resources, including links to many of the tools and books I've mentioned. You can also ask questions that will be answered on our blog.

Good luck, and I look forward to hearing your success story.

Made in the USA
Middletown, DE
17 September 2016